JOY COMPASS

Thriving and Navigating Uncertain Times

Michelle-Renée

Copyright 2025 by Michelle-Renee Johnson

All rights reserved.

No part of this book may be reproduced, stored in a retrieval system, or transmitted in any form or by any means—electronic, mechanical, photocopying, recording, or otherwise—without the prior written permission of the author, except in the case of brief quotations embodied in critical articles and reviews and certain other noncommercial uses permitted by copyright law.

You may notice a recurring theme of joy throughout this book. This is intentional—true joy is a thread woven into the fabric of our lives, not confined to a single moment or event. Its essence is ever-present, flowing through various seasons of life.

Easy-to-Read Version (ERV) – Copyright © 2006 by Bible League International. Used by permission. All rights reserved.

New International Version (NIV) – Scripture taken from THE HOLY BIBLE, NEW INTERNATIONAL VERSION®. Copyright © 1973, 1978, 1984, 2011 by Biblica, Inc.™ Used by permission. All rights reserved worldwide.

The Message (MSG) – Scripture taken from THE MESSAGE, copyright © 1993, 2002, 2018 by Eugene H. Peterson. Used by permission of NavPress. All rights reserved.

New Living Translation (NLT) – Scripture quotations are taken from the Holy Bible, New Living Translation, copyright © 1996, 2004, 2015 by Tyndale House Foundation. Used by permission of Tyndale House Publishers, Inc., Carol Stream, Illinois 60188. All rights reserved.

Christian Standard Bible (CSB) – Scripture taken from the Christian Standard Bible®, Copyright © 2017 by Holman Bible Publishers. Used by permission. Christian Standard Bible® and CSB® are federally registered trademarks of Holman Bible Publishers. All rights reserved.

Dedication

To my beautiful granddaughter Aniyah:

You are a spark of... JOY!

May you always live in the fullness of joy, and may the joy of the Lord be your strength!

Acknowledgements

To Abba Father: Your overwhelming and never-ending love is the foundation of my being. Everything I am belongs to You. I love You with all my heart and always will.

To my Dad: Thank you for your unconditional love that led me straight into the arms of our Heavenly Father, where true joy resides. For this, I am eternally grateful.

To my Mom: Your love and countless prayers, many of which I may never truly know, are the reason miracles come true. You are a blessing beyond words.

To my children, Andrew, Zachary, and Desiree, and Grandchildren: Thank you for bringing so much joy to my life. May the Lord bless you to know His joy beyond comprehension.

To all my covenant sisters in Christ (you know who you are): Thank you for your prayers and for pushing me to keep going when I didn't believe it was possible. Having you by my side means the world to me.

To my Pastor, Apostle Joshua Giles: Your mentorship and the truth you spoke into my soul ignited the spark to believe in the impossible. Connecting with your ministry has changed my life, and for that, I am forever grateful.

I am deeply grateful to Pastor Sam Mabanag and Pastor John Harris for your encouragement and the prophetic words spoken over my life. I trust in the Father's faithfulness to fulfill them for His glory!

To my editors, Tanisha and Rachael: Thank you for taking my vision and bringing it to life with your creativity and professionalism. Your work has elevated this book to the next level, and I deeply appreciate it.

Finally, to my readers: Thank you for your interest and support. May you be full of joy always!

Contents

Introduction 1

Chapter 1: The Nature of Joy 9

Chapter 2: Cultivating Joy 27

Chapter 3: How to Stay Joyful 52

Chapter 4: Obstacles to Joy 66

Chapter 5: A Joyful & Grateful Heart 92

Chapter 6: Joyful Relationships 113

Chapter 7: The Essence of Joy 131

Chapter 8: Joy in Giving 151

Chapter 9: Joy and Resilience 166

Chapter 10: The Key to Joy 182

Introduction

True Joy: Joyful Living Despite Chaos

In a world where chaos seems to be served daily complete with a side of uncertainty and a sprinkle of turmoil—the pursuit of joy can feel like searching for a needle in a haystack. Between the onslaught of bleak news, the relentless challenges of everyday life, and the ever-growing to-do list, it's easy to wonder if joy is reserved for fairy tales or the "perfect" lives portrayed on Instagram. "Spoiler alert: those lives aren't as perfect as they appear!"

Yet, amidst all the noise and confusion, there is a beacon of hope—a promise of joy that remains steadfast, no matter what's happening around us. This isn't some pie-in-the-sky, wishful thinking kind of joy. This joy comes from Scripture giving us the strength to thrive even in chaos. And yes, this kind of joy is real. It's available to anyone willing to embrace it, even if that embrace begins as a tentative hug rather than a full-on bear squeeze.

If you've picked up this book, I can probably guess you're here for one of two reasons. Maybe you're feeling like the world is spinning out of control, and you're hoping this book will provide some insights—or even a few secrets—on how to reclaim your joy. Or perhaps you've already discovered that sweet spot of joy and are determined to hold on to it for dear life.

Either way, welcome! We're about to embark on a journey together, one that will explore how to live in a place of continuous joy, even when life seems intent on testing your patience and sanity.

Now, let me be clear from the start: I'm not here to offer you a magic formula for a trouble-free life. (If I had that, I'd be on a yacht somewhere, sipping lemonade!) What I am here to do is share what I've learned about finding true joy—a joy that doesn't crumble when life gets tough. And where have I found this joy? It comes from putting my hope in the ultimate source of joy: the One who designed it, created it, and offers it freely to us all.

Let's be honest. Life on this planet we call Earth is anything but predictable. Things are constantly shifting, and it's easy to feel like we're stuck on a never-ending rollercoaster. But here's the good news: joy doesn't depend on the state of the world around us. It isn't held hostage by our circumstances. Instead, it's a gift—one that comes directly from a loving Father who specializes in turning our chaos into something beautiful.

The Bible, that ancient and ever-reliable guidebook, has much to say about joy. From the trials and triumphs of the Old Testament to the peaceful teachings of the New Testament, the message is clear and consistent: joy isn't tied to what's happening around us. It's tied to the One who is always with us, no matter what.

Take Psalm 16:11, for example: *"You make known to me the path of life; in your presence there is fullness of joy; at your right hand are pleasures forevermore."*

This verse beautifully reminds us that true joy is found in God's presence, even when the world around us is in chaos. It's a joy that surpasses understanding, anchoring us in His unfailing love.

Now, let's pause for a moment and think about how joy is typically defined. The dictionary describes joy as:

A feeling of great delight or happiness caused by something exceptionally good or satisfying.

A deep feeling of contentment or happiness.

Sounds lovely, doesn't it? But did you notice something? According to this definition, joy appears to be just an emotion—a reaction to something good happening in our lives. But what if I told you that true joy goes much deeper than that? What if I told you that true joy can only be found in Jesus, the ultimate source of all real joy? Without this understanding, we might find ourselves on a never-ending quest for happiness—one as fleeting as a summer breeze.

Throughout Scripture, we see countless examples of individuals who chose joy despite overwhelming odds.

Think of Abraham, who trusted God's promises even when they seemed impossible, or Esther, who found the courage to stand up for her people in the face of danger. After losing her parents and being raised by her uncle, Esther was brought to the royal palace as part of a search for a new queen following the former queen's dismissal.

Compelled by royal decree to participate in this selection, she was chosen by God, strategically positioned, and shown favor by the king, ultimately enabling her to protect her people. At a pivotal juncture, Esther faced a significant decision: remain concealed and hope her identity would not be discovered or take the risk of approaching the king uninvited—an act punishable by death—in order to seek deliverance for her people. She chose to call for a three-day fast among her community before presenting herself to the king, declaring, "If I perish, I perish." Esther's courage and faith resulted in a favorable outcome, as she successfully advocated for her people's survival. This ultimately brought joy to a whole nation because of her obedience to risk everything to save them.

These stories are more than just inspiring tales—they are powerful testimonies to the extraordinary strength that comes from choosing joy in the midst of chaos.

Esther found joy—not just for herself, but for an entire nation—during one of the most dangerous and unpredictable situations imaginable. Her story reminds us that even when life feels like it's spinning out of control, joy is possible if we're willing to trust God's plan.

Now, don't get me wrong. We've all experienced moments of happiness that had nothing to do with a Bible verse or a church sermon. And yes, sometimes what seemed like joy came from things we knew we shouldn't have been doing. (You know what I'm talking about!) But here's the problem: those fleeting moments of happiness often lead us down a dead-end road, leaving us searching for something more.

When you dig a little deeper, you may find that the most profound joy you've ever experienced has a connection to Jesus—whether you realized it at the time or not.

If you don't see that connection just yet, don't worry. My hope is that by the end of this book, you'll be able to look back and notice a thread running through your life—a thread that leads you to the source of all true joy. He is the One who made you, adores you, and is ready to fill your life with a joy that doesn't waver, no matter what.

The chapters in this book feature recurring themes and writings that emphasize how joy is intricately woven into our lives, often in ways we may not yet recognize. My hope is that whenever you find yourself lacking the joy you need, you can easily turn to a specific theme or chapter and discover the inspiration to reignite the spark of joy within you. This book is designed to serve as a devotional for those tough moments in life—when you feel discouraged or find yourself struggling to reclaim your joy.

So, let's dive in together. Let's explore how we can live in a place of extraordinary joy every single day, even when the world around us feels like it's falling apart. My prayer is that as you read these pages, you'll encounter Jesus in a new and powerful way. May your relationship with Him grow deeper as you sit at His feet, soaking in the incredible joy He offers to those who seek Him.

Let's Pray:

Heavenly Father,

We ask that You meet with us as we journey through this book. Help us understand the truth that You alone are the source of all true joy. Draw us closer to You as we seek to know You more. Teach us to trust Your process, and may Your joy become complete in us, overflowing to everyone we encounter.

Amen.

The theme of this book centers on the Fruit of the Spirit, where true joy is cultivated. As Galatians 5:22-23 says:

"But the fruit of the Spirit is love, joy, peace, patience, kindness, goodness, faithfulness, gentleness, self-control; against such things there is no law."

In Galatians, we learn that joy is one of the qualities God develops in us as believers. As we walk out our faith in the Lord, the essence of joy grows in our lives, maturing as we become more like Jesus.

So, how's your essence of joy today? Have you noticed the joy in your life growing or shrinking over time? Here's the good news: it's not up to you to produce this fruit of the spirit. It's the work of the Holy Spirit in you as you trust and rest in Him. He is the one who cultivates joy through the trials and tests we face.

And here's the surprising part: those trials—moments that often feel like the opposite of joy—are the very things that help produce it. As the Apostle Paul reminds us in Romans 5:3-4: *"Not only that, but we rejoice in our sufferings, knowing that suffering produces endurance, and endurance produces character, and character produces hope, and hope does not put us to shame, because God's love has been poured into our hearts through the Holy Spirit who has been given to us."*

Now, that's something to get excited about! Even the chaos in our lives is being worked for our good. I know—it sounds a bit wild to find joy in the middle of struggles. But when we look back, we often realize that the hardest times were the seasons that helped us grow the most.

As we move forward together in this book, we'll dig deeper into what Scripture says about joy. We'll explore practical ways to cultivate a life of joy, even when the world feels out of control. My prayer is that this journey will bring you encouragement, enlightenment, and empowerment.

May you discover the joy of the Lord that lives within you through the Holy Spirit. May you find that this joy is, indeed, your greatest source of strength.

So, buckle up—we're about to embark on an adventure, a joy-filled one. And no matter how chaotic things get, remember this: joy is always within reach. Let's discover it together.

CHAPTER 1

The Nature of Joy

The True Source

You might be wondering how this book could help you find deeper, lasting joy—and why I feel qualified to talk about it in the first place.

Well, let me tell you, life has given me a front-row seat to grief, loss, and suffering, just like many of you. But here I stand, more grateful and humbled than ever. And let me say this—it's the joy of the Lord that held me together like spiritual duct tape through it all.

Take, for example, the day I had to drive home, heart shattered into a million pieces, eyes so full of tears I could barely see the road. Why? Because yet another attempt to pick up my sons for their court-ordered visit had failed. Let me paint the picture for you: I'd made the mistake of letting them live with their dad without going through legal channels, thinking it would help him with his back child support. Fast forward a year, and suddenly I owed him child support, and my visitation rights were being challenged. Yep, the tables had turned, and the battle began—especially because I wasn't allowed to see my boys anymore, just to keep his case airtight.

That day is seared into my memory. It's the kind of heartbreak that drains joy from even the most resilient person. But in that moment, as I sat there feeling broken beyond repair, the love of the Father met me right where I was. I can still hear His gentle voice saying, "You're going to have to trust Me. I don't force My children to come to Me, and you can't force yours to come to you. Rest in Me, and I'll make it as if this never happened." To this day, I'm still trusting Him for that promise. And let me tell you, I've seen glimmers of hope—enough to keep praising Him for His faithfulness. Oh, and those funds I owed for back child support because he had now gained legal custody of my sons. Well, the Lord turned that all around in my favor. What started out as $14,000 soon accrued to over $50,000 in a few years. That's a mind-blowing amount of money in such a short amount of time, but God was faithful because I had done nothing wrong. I wanted the best for my sons and thought I had made a sound decision, and I just wanted time with them. After years of court proceedings and fighting for my legal rights. I started receiving some small deposits into my checking account when I called to inquire why these funds were coming to me. I was told it was money that was owed to me from their father, but I assured them that I actually owed him money. So, they check the records, and sure enough, he also owed me. The kicker in this story is... I owed him $50,000, but he owed me $52,000. Imagine that? My mouth dropped open in amazement. Only God could have done something like this. And, because he owed me more, I called him and told him I'd cancel the $2000 he owed. He agreed, and that debt was resolved, and I give God all the glory! That $50,000 debt was canceled in one moment, and it was indeed a joyful day, hallelujah!

Then there was the time a close friend lost her son to cancer. I remember all the trips with her and personally taking Daniel to doctor's appointments, all while trusting in God's faithfulness to heal him. I remember praying for him one day, because he had a tennis ball-sized growth on his knee. As we prayed, we noticed a visible reduction to about half the size. Even the doctors were shocked, asking what happened at his follow-up appointment. We told them we prayed, and God had done this; they told us to keep praying then, yes, prayer works miracles. As he continued his treatments faithfully. We prayed, believed, and hoped for his healing, but God chose to take him home. I can tell you that the sadness I personally experienced from this loss, after so much hope, shook me to my core and even challenged my faith. For both my friend and me, it was truly indescribable. Losing a child—no matter the circumstances—is one of the hardest things a person can endure. It's completely out of the natural order of things. Yet, through her grief, my friend showed a strength that still amazes me. To this day, she carries a joy and peace that are rare and beautiful.

And how could I forget driving to San Diego to visit my brother Michael? He had been lost in the prison system after being wrongly accused, which is a whole other story. But our family had not been able to locate him for several years. We received a call one day from a prison warden, that he was at a nursing facility, and Doctors had given him just two days to live after finding two brain tumors and being diagnosed with Sarcoidosis.

They informed our family that we should come and visit him as soon as possible. When we arrived, he was unresponsive, and honestly, I barely recognized him. He had a tracheotomy in his throat, helping him breathe, and he was barely moving. He just didn't look like my brother at all, to be honest. But God whispered, "Pray resurrection life over him." So, we did. That night, life returned to his body. I can still remember him looking into my mom's eyes and calling out "Mama" with tears coming down his cheeks. He was so happy to see us. We would later learn that he had to scream with all his might for us to be able to hear him say anything because of the tracheotomy. They told us the tracheotomy would never be removed because it had been in too long. But God had a different plan. Michael went on to live three and a half more years. The tracheotomy came out at one point, and he was able to breathe on his own. I have a picture of him holding a picture to review it on his own and smiling as he recognized those in the image, and he could respond with gestures; he was defying every medical prediction. Seeing these miracles brought so much joy to our family for that season, even though Michael eventually went on to be with the Lord. When life shifts in unpredictable ways, we can still find the joy thread through it all.

Of course, we can't forget 2020—the year that felt like a bad plot twist. The pandemic hit hard, and the losses piled up. For me, it was like a generational roll call: parents, stepparents, grandparents, aunts, uncles, cousins—all gone in just three years. Rising from that kind of loss can feel impossible at times. But if you're still here (and you are, because you're reading this), let's just say: God isn't done with you yet. The Lord wants to take all our pain and discomfort and turn it into something beautiful, if we'll let him. We'll discuss how a little later. But for now, please know that nothing is wasted that we go through or experience; the Father makes beautiful things out of the ashes.

I know this because I went through a very dark season in my life and battled with severe depression and anxiety. I remember not even being able to leave my house at one point, because fear had gripped my heart so strongly. It's not an experience I'd wish on anyone. Yet, looking back, I wouldn't trade those lessons for anything. Several years later, I learned about God's unrelenting love and deliverance for those who are bound with fear, which transformed my life completely. He will meet us at our lowest point and raise us up again. We are never alone when we have a relationship with the Father.

Finally, the fact that this book even exists is nothing short of a miracle. Why, you ask? Well, let's just say reading has never exactly been my strong suit. I was held back in the first grade because of it, and let me tell you, reading out loud in class felt like walking a tightrope without a safety net.

I knew I'd stumble over the words and end up embarrassed. And yep, that fear still tries to sneak up on me now and then.

It wasn't until one of my kids was diagnosed with dyslexia that the light bulb went on for me: Ohhh, so that's why reading always felt like a boxing match. Let's be real—writing a book is a daunting task for most people.

Add a dash of dyslexia, and you've got yourself a recipe for second-guessing every word.

But here's the thing: God told me, "I want you to write a book." And here we are—living proof that miracles still happen. Honestly, if He can use me to write this, there's nothing He can't do!

So, why am I sharing all this? Not because my life has been a bed of roses—far from it. I'm smiling and full of joy today because I've tasted the goodness of God. And if He can do it for me, He can do it for you. This book isn't about my life story; it's about how you can anchor yourself in joy, even when life turns upside down.

So, let's get started.

If I could capture the essence of pure joy, it would be a kaleidoscope of colors as vibrant as an iridescent rainbow after a summer storm. Imagine the air filled with amazing aromas of lilies and wildflowers alongside beautiful melodies so uplifting that your heart leaps in rhythm, all while the warmth of God's love wraps around you like a comforting blanket. As you dance with Jesus in pure delight, watching baby animals dart by, keeping time with every step. Meanwhile, being surrounded by smiling loved ones, singing in perfect harmony. And don't forget the gentle kiss of His sunlight on your face, bringing your complexion into a perfect glow that no earthly experience can rival.

That is one of my imaginative views of joy—pure, unshakable, and eternal.

But let's pause for a moment and discover how to have true joy here on planet earth, minus the daydreaming.

The True Source of Joy

The origin of true joy begins and ends with the Father. God is the ultimate source, the wellspring from which all joy flows. Can I get an "Amen?"

For centuries, humanity has searched far and wide for lasting joy, only to overlook what has been in plain sight all along—God Himself. This joy isn't fleeting or dependent on circumstances; it's a divine gift, rooted in our Creator and made complete through Jesus Christ.

Psalm 16:11 says:

"You make known to me the path of life; in your presence, there is fullness of joy; at your right hand are pleasures forevermore."

Did you catch that? In His presence, joy becomes full—overflowing, vibrant, and transformative. It's not just a temporary feeling but an unshakable reality that fills every corner of your soul.

Joy is a gift from God—a stunning expression of His boundless grace and infinite love. It's the light that pierces through the darkest corners of our hearts, guiding us toward redemption and renewal. As we embrace this divine joy, we uncover our true selves and the deeper meaning of our purpose: to love God, to love others, and to be a beacon of light in a world often shadowed by despair.

The Joy of Jesus

Jesus embodies this divine joy. In John 15:9-11, He says:

"As the Father has loved me, so have I loved you. Abide in my love. If you keep my commandments, you will abide in my love, just as I have kept my Father's commandments and abide in his love. These things I have spoken to you, that my joy may be in you, and that your joy may be full."

Jesus didn't merely wish for us to experience fleeting happiness. He prayed for us to be filled to the brim with joy—joy so radiant that it draws others closer to Him. Imagine living a life so joyful that people ask, "What's your secret?" and you can confidently reply, "It's the joy of my King!" That, my friend, is worth celebrating.

We ought to be the most joyful people on the planet because we carry the joy of the Creator within us. So, the next time life weighs you down and you're tempted to grumble about what's wrong in the world, remember this: Jesus has already prayed for your joy to be full—so full it catches the attention of the world.

It's time to let that joy shine and give the world something to marvel at!

Now, if you haven't experienced this kind of joy in your life, let me tell you—you're missing out on a wonderful gift that our Heavenly Father wants to give you.

Remember the momentous announcement in Luke 2:10-11 when Jesus was born? The angel said:

"Don't be afraid, for look, I proclaim to you good news of great joy that will be for all the people: Today in the city of David a Savior was born for you, who is the Messiah, the Lord."

When Jesus entered the world, He brought with Him a joy that has been available to all of us ever since. But here's the key: the joy He offers isn't just about fleeting happiness or feeling good. It's about discovering a deep, lasting peace and fulfillment that's rooted in our relationship with God—a joy that flows from knowing Jesus took our place on the cross, paid the price for our sins, and made a way for us to be reconciled with the Father.

So, let me ask you: Have you accepted this incredible gift? Have you returned to the Father through the sacrifice Jesus made for you? Here's the truth: every one of us has done things that separate us from God. Even as children, we quickly learn how to lie, disobey, and make choices that fall short of God's perfection. Yet, in His infinite love, God provided a solution before we even knew we needed one.

The Gift of Salvation

This joy begins with accepting the greatest gift of all—salvation through Jesus.

God, in His infinite love, provided a way for us to be reconciled to Him—through Jesus Christ.

Romans 6:23 reminds us:

"For the wages of sin is death, but the gift of God is eternal life in Christ Jesus our Lord."

That solution is Jesus—Yeshua Hamashiach—the One who bore the sins of the world, died in our place, and rose again, demonstrating that He is God. Jesus didn't just die for some of us; He died for all of us. Every sin you've ever committed—or ever will—is covered under the blood He shed on the cross on your behalf. Through His perfect life and sacrifice, we are no longer separated from God when we believe and put our trust in Yeshua/Jesus, the true source of all joy!

Without Jesus, we're left chasing after fleeting happiness that never truly satisfies. But when you accept the Father's gift by believing in His Son and embracing the truth that Jesus paid the ultimate price for your sins, you step into a new reality filled with pure joy, unshakable freedom, and eternal life.

Now, don't misunderstand—choosing to follow Jesus comes with a cost. It's not merely about saying a prayer at church and continuing with life as usual. Jesus made it clear that following Him means taking up your cross, which is a form of death. In other words, it's about surrendering your own plans, and living according to His will for your life —even when it requires sacrifice.

It's a decision that demands thoughtful consideration; it's not something to be walked into casually or without thoughtful consideration, for it is the most important choice you will ever make—one with eternal consequences.

A Call to Salvation

If you've never made the decision to follow Jesus, today is the day. The Bible says, *"Today is the day of salvation"* (2 Corinthians 6:2).

If you feel a stirring in your heart, a nudge from the

Holy Spirit, don't ignore it. God is calling you back to Himself. Take a closer look at your life and come back to the Father. I encourage you to respond.

You can pray right here and right now—a simple, heartfelt prayer to accept His gift of salvation. And when you do, heaven itself will rejoice over your decision. You'll become a new creation today! You will carry the DNA of your Father in heaven and have the privilege of being called a child of God. Because you will be adopted into God's family. 2 Corinthians 5:17 says, *Therefore, if anyone is in Christ, he is a new creation; the old has passed away, and see, the new has come!* You will be stepping into a life filled with complete joy, unshakable hope, and eternal peace.

Complete Joy

Heavenly Father,

Thank You for Your goodness and unfailing love. I humbly acknowledge that I have fallen short of Your holy standards and have done things that are not pleasing to You—things You call sin. These sins have separated me from Your presence and love. Today, I come before You with a repentant heart, asking for Your forgiveness.

I want to turn away from everything that displeases You and live a life that honors and glorifies You. I recognize that because You are holy, no sin can remain in Your presence. But in Your mercy, You sent Jesus to take my place, dying on the cross for my sins as a sinless and perfect sacrifice. Thank You, Jesus, for Your incredible love and obedience to the Father on my behalf.

Today, I choose to lay all my sins at Your feet and ask that the blood of Jesus cleanse me completely. I believe in His sacrificial death, burial, and resurrection, and I accept the new life He offers. Help me to walk in a way that brings you honor and joy to Your heart. Fill me with Your goodness and joy as I commit to follow Your plans, all the days of my life.

I understand that following You will cost me something, probably everything, but I am ready to surrender it all because I trust Your perfect will. I invite you, Holy Spirit, to guide me, direct my paths, and lead me into a deeper relationship with You. Thank You for Your promise to never leave me or forsake me.

In Jesus' mighty name, Amen.

If you prayed that prayer sincerely, welcome to the family of God! You are now a son or daughter of the MOST HIGH GOD, the KING of GLORY—hallelujah! Heaven is rejoicing with you, and I'm celebrating with you, too.

Your journey with the Father is just beginning, and it's going to be an incredible adventure as you discover more of His love, grace, and purpose for your life. The Bible reminds us to become disciples of Jesus, living according to His teachings and reflecting His love in everything we do.

As you spend time in prayer and reading His Word, you'll grow closer to Him and deepen your faith. You can start with the book of "JOHN" to learn more about the life of Jesus. But don't walk this journey alone! I encourage you to find a Bible-believing church where you can connect with other followers of Jesus who will encourage and support you.

JOY NUGGET

Biblical joy is not absent from pain or based on our circumstances; **it's rooted in trusting…God's perfect will for our lives** and about being anchored to the unchanging love of Christ. Because in His presence, there you will find the fullness of Joy!

DRAWING CLOSER

We don't have to pretend to be joyful when we're not; instead, we can invite Jesus into our present reality. He can handle our emotions. Ask the Lord how He wants to bring more joy into your life and circumstances.

This week, meditate on Psalm 16:11 and ask yourself: "Am I living in the fullness of joy God offers?" Write down what the Father reveals as you draw near to Him. Let His presence fill your heart with peace, gratitude, and unshakable joy.

Scripture Reading (Psalm 16)

Closing Section with QR Code

To start this amazing adventure with the Lord … please use the QR code below. Welcome home!

*The **JOY** of the **LORD** is my strength!*

Nehemiah 8:10 (CSB)

Reflection & Revelation to Remember

CHAPTER 2

Cultivating Joy

Creating Habits of Joy

As believers, we have a secret advantage when it comes to cultivating joy in our lives. Want to know what that is? We have a Helper—an ever-present guide living within us: the Holy Spirit. That's right, the Holy Spirit is our personal trainer in joy, leading us, guiding us, and reminding us of all the good things God has in store for us. The Holy Spirit is like a compass that guides us through life and helps us make decisions based on wisdom and God's will for our lives. He wants to direct us into a life filled with peace and joy, no matter how chaotic the world becomes.

However, like anything worthwhile, cultivating joy requires effort. It's not like flipping a switch; it's more like planting a garden. We need to create habits—daily, purposeful choices—that allow joy to grow in our lives. At first, creating these habits might feel like pulling weeds (okay, maybe that's just me and my lack of a green thumb), but over time, these habits become second nature. They help us find order in the chaos and, more importantly, experience joy even when life throws us a curveball.

Here are a few ways to start cultivating joy. As we practice these, we'll find our joy increasing day by day.

1. Prayer and Meditation

Let's start with the basics: reading and meditating on the Word. Now, before you roll your eyes and think, "Well, of course," hear me out. I know this seems like a no-brainer, but in today's fast-paced, technology-driven world, the simple act of quiet reflection has become a lost art. The world tells us to "look within" and meditate on ourselves, but Scripture provides a much better way. Check out Philippians 4:8:

"Finally, brothers and sisters, whatever is true, whatever is honorable, whatever is just, whatever is pure, whatever is lovely, whatever is commendable—if there is any excellence, if there is anything worthy of praise—think about these things."

This verse essentially encourages us to get our minds off the junk thrown at us daily and focus on the good stuff. And let's be honest: with the news, social media, and the endless stream of negativity, it's easy to get dragged into the messiness. But by meditating on God's Word and focusing on His goodness, we can shift our perspective and let joy back in.

Jesus makes it clear that staying connected to Him is crucial. In John 15:5, He says, *"I am the vine; you are the branches. The one who remains in me and I in him produces much fruit."* Guess what one of the attributes of this fruit is? That's right—joy!

When we spend time with God through prayer, we're not just ticking off a religious to-do list; we're plugging into the ultimate source of joy.

John 15:10-11 says it best: *"If you keep my commands, you will remain in my love, just as I have kept my Father's commands and remain in His love. I have told you this so that my joy may be in you, and your joy may be complete."*

Praying not only brings us peace in a chaotic world, but it also helps us understand God's will for our lives. Living in alignment with His will brings deep, lasting joy. When we know who we are and why we were created, life becomes less about surviving and more about thriving.

Plus, taking time to slow down, quiet our hearts, and notice the little things—like a stunning sunset or the song of early morning birds—gives joy a chance to rise within us. Sometimes, joy is as simple as paying attention to the world around us and recognizing God's hand in it all.

2. Gratitude: Having a Thankful Heart

If joy had a best friend, it would undoubtedly be gratitude. Nothing sparks joy faster than a thankful heart. As believers, we have an abundance of reasons to be grateful! While the world may overlook life's small blessings, we recognize that our Heavenly Father is constantly working behind the scenes, orchestrating everything for our good.

Consider the comforting promise in Jeremiah 29:11:

"For I know the plans I have for you," declares the LORD, "plans for peace and not for evil, to give you a future and a hope."

That verse feels like a warm, reassuring hug from God, reminding us that He's got everything under control. His plans are filled with hope and joy, and we can rest assured that all He does is for our ultimate good. When we embrace this truth, how can we not be grateful?

But here's the key about gratitude: it takes practice. Like joy, it's a habit we need to cultivate. A grateful heart shifts our focus from what we don't have to what we do have. It transforms a mindset of lack into one of abundance. And as we focus on the blessings in our lives, something amazing happens—those blessings seem to multiply! Gratitude is like a snowball rolling downhill; it builds momentum, and soon, your heart is overflowing with joy.

Psalm 118:24 captures this beautifully:

"This is the day the Lord has made; I will rejoice and be glad in it."

Every single day is a gift, and that alone is reason enough to leap for joy!

Even when life gets challenging (and let's be honest, which we know, it often does), gratitude reminds us that God is still in control. He is still good, despite what's going on around us or how we feel, and He is still working all things out for our benefit.

So, the next time you feel overwhelmed, take a moment to reflect on the blessings in your life. Start listing the things you're grateful for, and watch as your heart begins to feel lighter, your spirit lifts, and joy starts to shine through.

3. Studying Scripture

If prayer is like plugging into the power source, then studying Scripture is like learning how to wield that power. Let's face it: With so many distractions in our fast-paced lives, many of us have gotten a little lazy when it comes to diving into the Word. Between podcasts, YouTube, and our favorite preachers, it's easy to rely on someone else's interpretation of Scripture instead of digging into it ourselves. I'll be honest—I've been guilty of this laziness, too. But I've had to rely on God's grace to help me grow in this area.

One thing is certain: the Bible isn't just another book. It's living and active—it's God's way of speaking directly to us, right here, right now. 2 Timothy 2:15 encourages us:

"Study and do your best to present yourself to God as one approved, a worker who has no reason to be ashamed, accurately managing and skillfully teaching the word of truth."

When we study Scripture, we come to know God's heart. We learn about His character, His promises, and His incredible love for us. The more we know about Him, the more joy we experience.

The Bible tells us that Jesus is the Word, meaning that when we read the Bible, we're spending time with Him—and that's where true joy is found.

As we grow more familiar with Scripture, we're also better equipped to share the joy and love of God with others. Let's be honest—there's witnessing someone learn about the love of Jesus for the first time and deciding to receive His free gift, because we shared this Good News, will light up our lives and theirs.

So, if you haven't already, create a new habit to study the Bible, hopefully daily. Start small—maybe a few verses or a chapter a day—and watch how God begins to speak to you through His Word. The more time you spend with Him, the more joy will naturally overflow from your life. And if reading isn't your thing, don't worry—there are plenty of Bible apps and audio versions that make it easier than ever to soak in the Word. The method you choose isn't as important as creating a new habit that allows you to have more time and space to soak in the word. The Father loves to spend time with us, and He will even begin to reveal His secrets to you as you draw closer to him. (1 Corn 2:10).

4. Kindness: Sharing Joy with Others

Here's the beautiful thing about joy: the more you share it, the more it grows. Have you ever noticed how joy is contagious? When you're feeling joyful, it tends to spread to the people around you. God's desire is for us to be so full of His joy that we can't help but pass it on to others.

One of the best ways to cultivate joy in your own life is by intentionally bringing joy to others. Random acts of kindness that release joy wherever we are. I'm reminded of a time when the Lord prompted me to leave an extra-large tip for a waitress one day. Before my friend and I could leave the restaurant, she shared how she was short on her rent and prayed for something to happen so she would have enough. I share this not for my benefit, but to highlight that our obedience to the promptings of God may just spark joy in someone else's situation and be an answer to prayer. It doesn't have to be grand gestures—it could be as simple as offering a word of encouragement, surprising someone with a small gift, or just being there for a friend who needs to talk. When we take our focus off ourselves and look for ways to lift others up, we often find that our own joy increases in the process.

Remember, we're called to be light in a world filled with darkness. And nothing brightens the world quite like the joy of the Lord shining through us. Kindness will be noticed when released in our culture today, because many have become so focused and distracted by social media and technology rather than human interaction. It seems we have started to lose our need for personal connection with one another. However, God has not designed us to be isolated; he wants us to stay connected to one another. Kindness is His design; it's the way we can stay connected. It requires a recipient to be kind; therefore, we need someone to release kindness to, which helps us stay connected. Don't fall for the lie that we don't need each other, because we do. And being a kind individual is how you can easily spread more joy and love in this distracted world.

5. Fellowship: The Joy of Togetherness

Fellowship is one of the beautiful gifts of the Christian walk that often gets overlooked in our fast-paced, "I can do it myself" culture. Yet, engaging with other believers and sharing our faith journeys isn't just a nice idea—it's essential. Not only does it encourage and strengthen us, but it also fosters joy and builds lifelong relationships that make life richer and more meaningful.

When we connect with other believers, we create a community where we can find support in times of need. It's like having a team of spiritual cheerleaders who uplift us when we're down and celebrate our victories with us. I had a situation arise that I thought was going to take me out. I was really struggling, by myself, thinking I would get through it, but I seemed to grow more and more depressed as each day passed. You see, one of my children was not responding to any calls or text messages from me or anyone else in our family, and no one knew where he was for a period of about 7 months or so. The challenge was that where he lived had just been deemed a disaster area because of widespread fire taking over the region, and it wasn't just him I was concerned about, but his wife and children as well. So not knowing they were safe was a bit much for my heart. I cried out to the Lord for reassurance, but He was silent, and no answers seemed to be coming. Being the creative person that I am, my imagination ran wild with possibilities, and not all of them were good if you know what I mean…All I knew to do was to say, "Help me, Jesus."

Finally, I decided to humble myself and share the burden with some sisters in Christ that I minister with, and they banded together to pray with me. Can I tell you the burden I was carrying was lifted the very next day? Wow, why had I waited so long to ask for help and reach out to the community? Thank God, I did. I felt a surge of renewed energy and hope, which enabled me to function somewhat normally again; the dark cloud of despair lifted and was replaced with strength and peace. Not only that, but shortly thereafter, I got news that my son had called his father and was alive. Can I tell you joy hit my heart like a lightning bolt! Our Heavenly Father knows what we need, especially our need for each other; it's more than we realize, at times. I pray you recognize the need for other believers in your life. How we need each other to walk through life together before tragedy. Fellowship keeps us aligned with God's perfect plan for our lives. And let's not forget, when we gather together, we become conduits of the Father's love, allowing it to flow through us to others.

Jesus said in John 15:12-13: *"This is my command: Love one another as I have loved you. No one has greater love than this: to lay down his life for his friends."* Jesus set the ultimate example of sacrificial love when He laid down His life for us on the cross. While most of us won't be called to literally give our lives for someone else, we can still follow His example by loving others with selfless devotion. This kind of fellowship—where we invest in others without expecting anything in return—is where true joy is found.

Hebrews 12:2 reminds us to: *"keep our eyes on Jesus, the pioneer and perfecter of our faith. For the joy that lay before him, he endured the cross, despising the shame, and sat down at the right hand of the throne of God."* Jesus found joy in fulfilling His mission, even though it involved immense suffering. And while we might not be asked to go to such extremes, we can find joy in loving and serving others, especially when it's difficult. In the end, those relationships often bring the greatest rewards.

As we build meaningful connections in this season, let's stretch ourselves—just as Jesus did—to bear one another's burdens. Trust that as we do, the Father will pour even more of His amazing joy into our lives.

6. Serve Others: The Joy of Giving

Serving others might sound countercultural in a world where the motto often seems to be, "What's in it for me?" But that's exactly why it's so powerful. When life becomes all about us, we lose sight of what truly matters—and we miss out on the incredible joy that comes from helping others.

At first glance, it might seem like the person receiving the help benefits the most. But look closer, and you'll find that the person who serves often experiences the greatest joy. That's why Jesus said, *"It's more blessed [and brings greater joy] to give than to receive"* (Acts 20:35).

Think back to a time when you did something kind for someone without expecting anything in return.

Remember the joy on their face? And think about how it made you feel.

That's the kind of joy Jesus is talking about—a deep, fulfilling joy that comes from serving others.

In today's world, it's easy to get wrapped up in our own needs and problems. But studies have shown that people who focus on serving others often feel less depressed and more fulfilled. There's something about helping and serving others that takes our attention off our own burdens and redirects our energy for the good. Have you ever noticed that when you're depressed, your thoughts have been on yourself and your needs or wants? By shifting our thoughts onto others, sometimes that's all it takes to lift our burden, even if only for a little while. Because the enemy can't successfully continue with his whispering lies of despair in our lives, when our attention is focused on helping someone else have a more joy-filled day. So, when you're feeling down, try shifting your focus outward. Help a neighbor, lend a hand to a friend, or even offer a kind word to someone in need. You might be surprised by how much joy it brings into your own life.

Hebrews 10:24-25 encourages us to:

"Think about each other to see how we can encourage each other to show love and do good works. We must not quit meeting together, as some are doing. No, we need to keep on encouraging

each other. This becomes more and more important as you see the Day getting closer."

As the world grows more chaotic, sticking together and serving one another becomes even more important. Just like in those old movies where neighbors relied on each other, serving builds a sense of community and shared joy. Serving others isn't just a kind gesture—it's essential to living a life filled with joy, especially as the days grow darker. We are on the cusp of seeing the ACT 2 church. We're those who followed the Way, had everything in common, and no one had need of anything. They sold all their possessions and pooled all their resources together, and worked together with real unity. This is the heart of God, and I believe we will see a true resurgence of this type of community in the ecclesia. The Father desires for us to be one, with one heart and one mind, resembling who He is in the earth. So close and connected with our brothers and sisters in Christ that the world will notice a difference and desire to know our God at a greater capacity. Let's be people who stick together…for real. Showing love through prayer, serving one another's needs both financially and practically, using our gifts as needs arise.

7. Forgiveness: The Joy of Letting Go

Forgiving someone can be one of the hardest things we're called to do, especially when the hurt runs deep. It's easy to say the words, "I forgive you," but truly letting go in your heart is another matter entirely. Yet, forgiveness is crucial—not just for the other person, but for our own well-being.

In Matthew 18:21-22, Jesus tells Peter to forgive not just seven times, but seventy times seven. If we're being truthful, by the third time someone repeats the same offense, many of us feel like we're at our limit. That's when we need God's grace the most to forgive as He has commanded. Jesus makes it clear that forgiveness isn't optional—it's essential. Why? Because unforgiveness doesn't only harm the one who wronged us; it hurts us, too. It can lead to bitterness, physical ailments, and even open doors to spiritual attacks. We are meant to be vessels of light and love, but unforgiveness invites darkness to take hold within us. Many people walk around carrying emotional and physical burdens that stem from unforgiveness. This is why it's so important to choose forgiveness, even when it's hard.

Jesus takes forgiveness so seriously that He says in Matthew 6:14-15, *"If you forgive others for the wrongs they do to you, then your Father in heaven will also forgive your wrongs. But if you don't forgive others, then your Father in heaven will not forgive the wrongs you do."* That's a pretty heavy statement, but it shows just how important forgiveness is to God.

Unforgiveness can rot us from the inside out. It breeds bitterness, which often leads to physical and emotional decay. However, when we choose to forgive—even when it's difficult—we release that heavy burden, allowing God's healing and joy to flow into our lives. Forgiveness isn't easy, but with the help of the Holy Spirit, it is possible. In the end, forgiveness brings freedom, and freedom is where joy truly resides.

The key to walking in forgiveness is rooted in genuine love, guided by the Holy Spirit. Honestly, I don't believe we can fully forgive another person without the Spirit's help. This truth is evident in today's culture, where anger seems to be on the rise. It's astounding how quickly a simple conversation can spiral into hostility, with just a few poorly chosen words escalating into a full-blown argument. These patterns of behavior appear to be manifesting more rapidly in recent times.

I believe this is because a heart burdened by unforgiveness often harbors anger and a short temper. These emotions become like uninvited guests, wreaking havoc on relationships and interactions. Yet, the Lord calls us to be holy people—set apart in this world—and that holiness should be reflected in how we engage with one another and those around us.

Walking in forgiveness is a choice that requires strength, grace, and a reliance on God. It's not just about letting go; it's about being transformed by His love so that we can live as His light in a dark world.

Col 3:12-13 says,

"God has chosen you and made you his holy people. He loves you. So, your new life should be like this: Show mercy to others. Be kind, humble, gentle, and patient. Don't be angry with each other, but forgive each other. If you feel someone has wronged you, forgive them. Forgive others because the Lord forgave you."

Walking in forgiveness helps us release anger and embrace patience, gentleness, and kindness. When we're consumed by anger, showing mercy to others becomes nearly impossible. However, with the help of the Holy Spirit, we can walk in forgiveness and, in turn, extend mercy to others just as we have received mercy.

When it's difficult to forgive, I've found that reflecting on all the forgiveness I've received from God—and from those I've hurt—humbles my heart. It reminds me to trust that God will make right what feels unjust. He is our vindicator, and nothing escapes His sight. Trusting the process of forgiveness—whether forgiving others or ourselves—ultimately leads to greater joy in our lives. It's a fight worth engaging in because joy is far sweeter than resentment.

When we struggle to forgive, it helps to remember all the ways God has shown us mercy. Reflecting on His grace softens our hearts and empowers us to release the burden of unforgiveness. As we forgive, we deepen our relationship with God and open the door to joy-filled connections with others.

8. Choose Joy: The Power of Free Will

One of the greatest gifts God has given us is free will—the ability to make choices. This gift can be used to glorify God or to bring harm to ourselves and others. The decisions we make have a profound impact, not only on our lives but also on the lives of those around us.

In Deuteronomy 30:19, *God says, "I call heaven and earth as witnesses against you today, that I have set before you life and death, the blessing and the curse. Therefore, you shall choose life in order that you may live, you and your descendants."*

God urges us to choose wisely because our choices can ripple through future generations. That's a sobering thought, having to consider that my choices today and how I spend my life will impact my children, grandchildren, and great-grandchildren who may not even be born yet...wow! No wonder the Lord says, **"Choose life."** Our current choices have a ripple effect and can lead to more blessings or curses on our families, whether we realize it or not. For example, if your dad was an alcoholic and you like to drink too, you can either decide...I know this is in my bloodline, but I want to change it and become a curse breaker in my family and create a blessing in its place, where my children will learn the importance of caring for our bodies and not bring harm upon them with excessive drinking. Making this one simple decision could lead to a lifetime of joy for generations. A life surrendered to God's will always leads to joy because, as Psalm 16:11 reminds us, *"You will teach me the right way to live. In your presence, there is fullness of joy."*

When we choose to stay close to the Father, we discover joy even in challenging circumstances. Joy doesn't mean we're always happy—it's about trusting the Father. This trust allows us to experience a joy that sustains us through life's toughest moments.

We can choose joy with our free will. Let's choose to live according to God's plan, not our own. Allowing him to guide us, teach us, and fill our lives with His abundant joy.

The more we walk in His ways, the more deeply we'll experience His joy—and the more we'll be able to share that joy with the world around us.

Cultivating joy isn't a one-time decision—it's a lifelong journey. The good news is that God has provided everything we need to live a life overflowing with joy. Through prayer, gratitude, studying Scripture, fellowship, serving others, praise and worship, forgiveness, exercising free will in alignment with His will, and sharing joy with others, we can establish habits that nurture joy in every season of life.

So, let's get to work! Let's cultivate these habits with intention, knowing that with each step we take, we are drawing closer to the Father—the ultimate source of all joy. And as we walk in His joy, we'll discover that even in the midst of life's chaos, we can live with peace, purpose, and, most importantly, unshakable joy.

9. Joy in Worship: Praise Him

One of the simplest and most delightful ways to experience joy in life is through worship. Worship isn't just about rituals or routines—it's about an intimate connection with God. It's the act of giving Him reverent honor, pouring out our hearts in gratitude, and acknowledging His greatness. Worship can take many forms: reading Scripture, singing, dancing, praying, or even sitting in silence to reflect on His goodness, just to name a few. Whether you're belting out your favorite worship song in the shower or talking to God during your commute, there's no limit to how you can engage with the Father.

Worship reminds us of our dependence on God. In the busyness of life, it's easy to try solving our problems on our own. But worship shifts our focus from our struggles to the One who holds the solutions. As Psalm 121:1-2 says, *"I lift up my eyes to the hills—where does my help come from? My help comes from the Lord, the Maker of heaven and earth."* Worship is a moment of surrender, a reminder that God is in control. It's like hitting the refresh button for our souls—a chance to acknowledge, "Oh right, I'm not the one running the universe here!"

Worship brings joy and hope. One of the most beautiful outcomes of worship is joy—real, deep, lasting joy. Worship changes the atmosphere around us. Have you ever had a day where everything feels gloomy, and all you want to do is curl up in bed? Try turning on worship music or reading a Psalm aloud. It's incredible how quickly the heaviness starts to lift.

Worship invites God's presence into our circumstances, and where His presence is, there is fullness of joy. It's like opening the curtains and letting sunlight flood into a dark room.

Worship is an act of trust. At its core, worship is about trust. It's saying, "God, I don't have all the answers, but I trust that You do." This trust is liberating. Instead of clinging tightly to our worries, we open our hands and let go, allowing God to step in. This act of trust fills our hearts with peace and joy.

I invite you, the next time you're feeling overwhelmed, down, or just plain tired, remember that worship is your secret weapon. Your worship is a type of surrender that allows the Father to step into your situation and fight on your behalf. When life gets overwhelming and you don't know what to do, a simple surrendering to trying to figure it all out on your own and worshipping instead might just turn your situation around. Worship is that powerful. It's the key to finding joy in every season of life. Sing a little louder, raise your hands, dance if you feel like it—worship is freeing, joyful, and most importantly, it brings us closer to the God who loves us more than we can imagine. And honestly, isn't that the best reason to praise Him?

JOY NUGGET

True joy must be cultivated with intention, it's like a garden that must be watered, weeds pulled, and then allowing the light of God's presence to saturate you with love so you can bear much fruit.

DRAWING CLOSER

Mediate on John 15:5, *I am the vine; you are the branches. The one who remains in me and I in him produces much fruit, because you can do nothing without me.*

Abiding in Jesus is how we allow our joy to grow; without abiding, the fruit of the Spirit remains the same. We must allow the Lord to uproot bitterness and unforgiveness in our hearts. We have to let go of our need to perform for his approval and learn to rest in him. True joy begins as we stay

connected to the true source of power and allow the Holy Spirit to work in and through us to accomplish His perfect will in our lives. Because the truth is, we can do nothing without him. He's inviting us to surrender and trust Him more today.

Scripture Reading (John 15)

Let's Pray:

Heavenly Father,

We thank You for cultivating joy in our hearts like a beautiful garden as we establish new habits to live out in our daily lives. As these seeds have been planted in our hearts, may You water them, allowing them to germinate, grow, and produce abundant fruit in our lives and the lives of those around us.

We are grateful that You are the vine dresser, and we are the branches You use on this earth to spread joy. Help us stay close to You and grow into all that You desire for us to be. May You receive all the glory!

Amen.

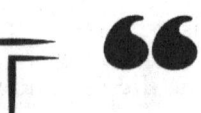

*This is the day the **LORD** has made; let's **REJOICE** and be glad in it.*

Psalm 118:24 (CSB)

Reflection & Revelation to Remember

CHAPTER 3

How to Stay Joyful

Every Day – Recognizing Joy Within

In today's fast-paced world, it's easy to get caught up in the chaos and miss the little blessings right in front of us. Endless to-do lists, work pressures, family responsibilities, and a constant flood of negative news make it no surprise that depression and anxiety are on the rise. But even in this whirlwind of busyness, there's a simple yet powerful practice that can transform our outlook and infuse more joy into our lives: gratitude.

Think about this: have you ever paused to truly savor the good things in your life? Something as straightforward as keeping a gratitude journal can be life-changing. When we write down what we're thankful for—even the small things—it shifts our focus from what's wrong to what's right. It's a daily reset, a chance to notice the blessings we often overlook.

Finding Joy in the Everyday

Over the years, I've discovered something simple yet profound: good things and bad things happen all the time. Simultaneously. If we don't make a deliberate effort to notice the good, we risk becoming so consumed by life's challenges that we overlook the blessings right before us.

It's like sitting down to a gourmet meal and focusing only on the fact that your napkin fell on the floor.

Now, I'm not saying there aren't seasons when life feels completely overwhelming. We've all been there. But even in those tough seasons, I've learned there's always something to be grateful for. Sometimes it's as basic as being alive and breathing. And let's be honest. Truthfully—on some days, that alone feels like a major accomplishment, doesn't it?

Honestly, when we're in the midst of overwhelming moments, it can feel like they'll never end. But most times we find out those moments are often fewer and farther between than they seem. For those of us who are blessed to live in relative comfort, it's humbling to remember that many people around the world are facing far greater challenges. This perspective can serve as a quick and powerful reminder to shift our focus back to gratitude.

The Cultural Blind Spot

In many parts of the world, particularly here in the U.S., we've become so accustomed to abundance that we risk taking it all for granted. We live in a culture where the relentless pursuit of "more" can blind us to the simple, beautiful moments happening around us every day. The beauty of a sunrise, the melody of birds singing in the morning, the laughter of children, or the warmth of a bowl of soup on a cold day—these everyday miracles can easily go unnoticed if we're not careful. And when we fail to notice them, we miss out on the joy they bring.

Gratitude keeps us grounded. It serves as a gentle reminder to savor life's simple pleasures. When we appreciate these small moments, they have a way of multiplying our joy, like a glimpse of the goodness God has waiting for us, this side of heaven. Imagine that!

Have you ever found yourself chasing after the next big thing? Maybe it's a promotion, a new car, or a bigger house. I know I have. I vividly remember a time when I was laser-focused on buying a new house. My sights were set on that goal, but in the process, I lost sight of the blessing of the home I was already living in. It wasn't until I stopped to consider those without a roof over their heads that I was jolted back to reality. The blessing wasn't in the house I wanted—it was in the house I already had. I had to stop and reflect on the abundance I was already living in and be grateful for the many blessings in my life. Most of us have more blessings than we recognize, or even worse, we simply take for granted. This keeps us in a state of striving and never coming to a place of rest, which most times leaves us living lives of great anxiety, we have created by wanting more. But true joy lies in being able to recognize all we have and being content in every situation.

It's so easy to get caught up in what we lack or what we're striving for, to the point we lose sight of the many blessings we already possess. And the truth is, life can change in an instant. One fire, one tornado, one hurricane, and everything could be gone.

That sobering thought is also a powerful reminder to be grateful for what we have right now.

Gratitude isn't just about recognizing what's in front of us; it's also about looking ahead with hope and joy. As we reflect on our blessings, we can rest in the assurance that God has even more in store for us. Because His plans for our lives are for good and not evil, to give us a hope and a future. (Jer 29:11).

Joy Through Worship and Music

We discussed earlier how worship and spending time in the presence of the Lord can transform our lives. Another powerful tool for cultivating joy is music—

especially worship music. If you've ever felt how music can change your mood, you know exactly what I'm talking about. Music has an incredible ability to shift the atmosphere. When we engage in worship through music, it does more than just lift our spirits; it draws us closer to the Father, where true joy resides.

Worship music invites us to focus on all the wonderful things God has done and is doing in our lives. It offers us a break from the noise of the world and the never-ending cycle of worries. When we sing praises, we step into a sacred space where we can leave our burdens behind and dwell in the presence of God.

I have had life-changing experiences during worship.

I've been in moments when the tangible presence of God was so strong that I didn't want to leave. That kind of joy lingers long after the music fades. If you haven't experienced this yet, I encourage you to ask God to meet you through worship. You won't regret it. In fact, you'll probably feel compelled to share it with everyone you know because some experiences are simply too good to keep to yourself!

The Role of Joy in Battling Depression and Anxiety

Now, let's pause for a moment. We live in a world where depression and anxiety are at epidemic levels. It seems like every other day there's a new tragedy or disaster unfolding on the news. For many, this constant stream of negative information can be overwhelming.

It's difficult to hold onto joy when we're constantly bombarded by the chaos of the world.

I'd like to share: joy and depression often stand in opposition to one another. Depression thrives in environments where hope and joy are pushed to the margins. It convinces us that the bad is bigger than the good, but that simply isn't true.

It's important to recognize the signs of depression—not just in ourselves but in the people we love. Here are a few common symptoms to watch for:

- Persistent feelings of sadness or anxiety.
- Loss of interest in activities that once brought joy.
- Irritability or restlessness.
- Trouble sleeping or sleeping too much.
- Changes in appetite.
- Physical symptoms like headaches or stomachaches.
- Difficulty concentrating.
- Feelings of worthlessness or guilt.
- Thoughts of self-harm or suicide.

If you or someone you know is experiencing these symptoms, it's crucial to seek help. Depression isn't something to be taken lightly, and no one should have to go through it alone.

It's also essential to understand that depression can happen to anyone. Even people who seem happy and successful on the outside can be battling depression on the inside. And it's not just a modern problem. King David, one of the most revered figures in the Bible, experienced deep moments of despair. He was honest about his struggles, and through his Psalms, we see how he continually turned to God for hope and joy.

The enemy loves to isolate us in our struggles, convincing us that we're the only ones feeling this way. But that's a lie.

Depression is something many people experience, and as we work through it, we can become a source of hope and healing for others.

I went through a season where I felt so hopeless, and I wasn't functioning well at all. The tricky part was that to most people, I looked perfectly fine. No one would have thought anything was actually wrong because I could go through all the motions of seeming okay. But inside, nothing could be further from the truth. I was so sad most of the time, and the things I used to love no longer mattered much. I couldn't put a name on it at the time, but I knew something was very wrong, and

I needed to find out what it was and fast. Emotions were raging, and when I talked to friends, they didn't have any answers.

I remember finding a program online that described what I was going through, and sure enough, it was anxiety and depression that were trapping me in this silent cage. I found out in this course that highly creative people can suffer from anxiety and depression at a greater level because of their imaginative minds, and they sometimes use their minds against themselves to come up with all kinds of scenarios they create that will never actually happen in real life. It can be a form of distraction to avoid what is really bothering us. So, if that's you and you're reading this, please know you could be using your God given gift in a negative way. The good news is that you can change your mind today. And rest assured, He wants you to understand how creative you really are, so you can be set free today.

Proverbs 17:22 says, *"A joyful heart is good medicine, but a crushed spirit dries up the bones."* Joy isn't just a nice-to-have— it's medicine for the soul. As we experience freedom and healing, we can become vessels of that joy for others.

A Joyful Heart Is Good Medicine

Our emotions are powerful, so powerful in fact, they can affect our immune systems both for good or bad.

Scientists have studied how joy and laughter have beneficial properties for our bodies in many ways.

Here are a few to take note of:

- Boost immune function.
- Lower blood pressure and heart rate.
- Trigger endorphin release (the Brain's natural painkillers).
- Reduce stress hormones like cortisol.
- Improve mood and resilience.

They have even begun to use laughter as a therapy in hospitals to induce positive emotions and to aid in recovery times for their patients.

(Neh 8:10) — *"The joy of the Lord is your strength"*

Joy has a way of giving us strength to keep going in the most trying times. And when we are not feeling well, we usually want only one thing to happen, that's to feel better.

That's when we have to remember that joy can bring us back to a place of wholeness. By creating a space for renewing your joy on a regular basis, you can bring strength to your body like medicine. This can be like a vitamin supplement that can sustain you in times when you are more vulnerable and stressed. Try creating a playlist of music that uplifts you, or saving your favorite comedic movies that make you laugh, so you can

Complete Joy

release the endorphins you need to get a bounce back. Just remember that joy and laughter have a way of boosting you and bringing strength to you in those days when you feel weary.

At the end of the day, joy is more than just a fleeting emotion. It's a gift from God, one that must be cultivated in our daily lives. Whether it's through keeping a gratitude journal, singing our hearts out in worship, or simply taking a moment to appreciate the small blessings around us, joy is always within our reach. When we choose to live with gratitude, joy, and laughter, we open the door for more joy to flood into our lives.

Let's be people who live with a heart of joy through laughter and gratitude. Let's be people who rejoice, even in the midst of chaos. Because when we live in gratitude, joy and laughter are sure to follow.

And if you're still not convinced, just imagine God looking down at us, smiling at all our frantic efforts to control everything, and saying, "Whenever you're ready to let me help, I'm right here." What a relief to know that joy is never far away—it's just a matter of remembering to look for it!

JOY NUGGET

We don't have to wait for Joy to find us; **we can choose to live in "JOY" daily.** When we align our hearts with God's truth, we will experience His protection and love in every circumstance. Which leads to a place of peace and joy!

DRAWING CLOSER

We have a choice daily to walk with Jesus or according to our own wills. When we choose His ways, He promises to guide us and lead us into all truth and give us the clear path to follow, the path he has already provided for us before the foundation of the earth. In this, we can rejoice in the Lord always. I will say it again: Rejoice! (Phil 4:4). Not because everything will be perfect and go exactly as we would like, but because He is with us and He's faithful and good and can be trusted. So, we can rest in Him by choosing joy everyday.

Scripture Reading (Phil 4)

Let's Pray:

Heavenly Father,

We thank You for the gift of joy that is ours for the taking. Today, we ask for help in recognizing the joy You have placed within us. We are grateful that we have access to this joy at any time, with the help of the Holy Spirit. Please remind us that we can run to You when we are overwhelmed by the cares of this world and all that distracts us from Your presence. We acknowledge that we need Your help to remain in a place of peace and joy.

Today, we invite You to live in us and through us as we rest in Your goodness and kindness toward us. We also pray for those in our families who may be suffering from depression and anxiety. We ask that You bring hope to their hearts now, in Jesus' name. If we are the ones in need of hope, help us to see You in everything that is draining us. We know this is not Your will or plan for our lives, so we thank You for guiding us to seek support and share our struggles, so we don't suffer alone. Thank You for hearing our cry today and for never leaving or forsaking us in our time of need. In Jesus' name, Amen.

> *Consider it a **GREAT JOY**, my brothers and sisters, whenever you experience various trials, because you know that the testing of your **FAITH** produces endurance.*
>
> James 1: 2-3 (CSB)

Reflection & Revelation to Remember

CHAPTER 4

Obstacles to Joy

With Joy

Life is full of obstacles and challenges that can easily derail us if we're not mindful, especially when we forget to keep Jesus at the center of it all. Isn't it remarkable how, amid the chaos and demands of life, we can become so focused on the problem at hand that we forget we have divine help? We often try to push through our challenges alone, ignoring the fact that the ultimate Helper, the Holy Spirit, is standing by, waiting for us to lean on Him.

Like a compass, He guides us to where we should be as we put our trust in Him. A compass is a navigational tool used to determine direction. It helps people find their bearings when traveling. Jesus/God's word is our guide, leading us on paths of righteousness. With the help of the Holy Spirit, we gain wisdom on how to maneuver through life by His grace and can eliminate pitfalls that delay progress and success in life. The word of God lets us know if we need to go north, south, east, or west. In addition, the compass has a magnet inside, and the Earth acts like a giant magnet with a magnetic field, with one end always pointing toward the magnetic North Pole.

This is symbolic of the Holy Spirit in the believer, that is, pulling us toward the ways we should follow if we will surrender our hearts and align them with his plans for our lives.

As we travel through life, we can sometimes veer off on paths and find ourselves in places we didn't plan to be in, but the Lord will never leave us or forsake us. He will guide us back to the right path when we repent and choose to follow Him again. The word is an infallible guide for our lives. Our feelings, opinions, and circumstances may change, but the Father's purposes and plans remain. He can be trusted; as we rest in Him, our joy will remain.

As Romans 8:28 reminds us:

"And we know that in all things God works for the good of those who love him, who have been called according to his purpose."

This verse is like a big, reassuring hug from God, isn't it? It reminds us that nothing in our lives goes unnoticed by our Father. Every trial, every difficult situation—He sees it all. What's more, He doesn't just see it; He allows it, knowing full well that we have the strength to handle it.

Now, we might argue with Him on that point from time to time, especially when we're in the thick of it. There are certainly moments when we feel extremely underprepared to face the trials before us. But when we look back on the hurdles we've already overcome—the ones we were convinced would be the end of us—we can see how those challenges stretched us, refined us, and made us stronger.

In hindsight, we often realize that they equipped us to help others in similar circumstances, sharing our story of how the Lord brought us through.

Think about it—God knew all along what we were capable of, even if we didn't. Our Father in heaven doesn't allow anything to enter our lives that He hasn't already equipped us to handle, even when we are unaware of our own strength.

Fire Refines Us

Just as gold must be purified in fire, so must we be refined through the trials of life. It's not exactly a pleasant thought—no one likes the idea of walking through the flames of adversity. Yet, it's in those fiery trials that we are purified, and there is simply no other way for that purification to happen. Sometimes, the only way to reveal the pure gold hidden beneath is through the pain and suffering of life's difficulties. The process of refining gold requires the removal of impurities (usually 99.9% pure or higher). First, they heat up and melt the gold. The furnace is turned up to almost 2000 degrees, then flux (like borax and soda ash) is added to help separate impurities, so they can be removed from the gold. The gold is dried and melted again and cast into bars or coins. This is how trials can feel in real life sometimes. Things can heat up to the point you don't think you can take it and just when we think we're about to break more pressure is added to cause all the remaining residue to come to the surface, until we are left with one of two choices, surrender to God's plans and trust the process or give up only to find we have returned to the same test again at a later date.

But if we surrender, the good news is He will cast us into the purified image of His Son and accomplish all He has for us.

The Book of Job gives us insight into this process. After losing nearly everything, Job clung to his faith in God, declaring in Job 23:10:

"Yet He knows the way I have taken; when He has tested me, I will emerge as pure gold."

The amazing part about Job's story is that he ended up with more than he lost at the end of the trial and the refinement. That's how good our Father is; he makes all the tests we go through work out for our benefit.

Embracing the trials we face can produce a version of ourselves that is stronger, wiser, and more compassionate than we ever imagined possible. While it may sound odd, when we reflect on the trials we've endured, many of us wouldn't change a thing. Those challenges shaped us, molding us into people with deeper faith, resilience, and a richer capacity for joy. In fact, James 1:2-4 even tells us to consider it joy when we face trials:

"Consider it pure joy, my brothers and sisters, whenever you face trials of many kinds, because you know that the testing of your faith produces perseverance. Let perseverance finish its work so that you may be mature and complete, not lacking anything."

Wait—pure joy in the middle of trials? Really, James? Are you serious? Apparently, Jesus knows something about the trials we face that we don't.

He understands that these challenges aren't just random acts of suffering. They serve a purpose, one that often leads to greater joy once we've come through the other side. The challenge for us is to endure the trial, trusting that our Father knows we will come out of it stronger and more mature. Jesus has already done the hardest part— dying on the cross for our salvation. Our part is to walk through the trials with the assurance that we are never alone and we will come out victorious.

The War Is Won, Even When the Battles Rage

Yes, we will experience suffering in this life. No one is immune to that. But it's comforting to know that while we may be fighting daily battles, the war has already been won. We can rest in the knowledge that we are more than conquerors through Christ. Every challenge we face is an opportunity to become stronger, to be further empowered by the One who holds the ultimate victory. This new perspective on life's obstacles can help us push through difficult times with a sense of purpose and strength that comes from knowing the Lord is by our side.

Isaiah 40:31 gives us this beautiful promise:

"But those who hope in the Lord will renew their strength. They will soar on wings like eagles; they will run and not grow weary; they will walk and not be faint."

This is an image of empowerment. When we trust in the Lord, we rise above our circumstances. He gives us the strength to run when we feel like collapsing and to keep walking when we're ready to give up. However, one thing remains: we have to ask for help. We have to admit that we're tired and that we can't do it all on our own. Only then can God renew our strength and help us soar above the chaos of life.

The Holy Spirit desires to partner with us to accomplish our God given assignments in the earth. The Father has graced all of us with different gifts and talents. These gifts are to be used while on the earth to do specific things that help other people and bring Him glory. When you start to recognize your real purpose and walk in it, the enemy will try to come after you to try to stop you. But, as you partner with the Lord, you will mount up with the wings of eagles and soar above the circumstances supernaturally. You will be able to do things you never thought possible. Because it is not you doing it, it's the empowerment of the Holy Spirit that anoints us to do the unimaginable. This ultimately brings glory to the Father and draws others to come to know him.

I shared earlier how it's a miracle that this book even exists, because in the natural, writing a book is the last thing I'd ever desire or want to do, and reading was not only hard but I'd avoid it whenever possible. Audio books were and still are my method of choice for reading books to this day. Me and the written word on paper had a love-hate relationship at one point. But it gets tricky out here when God has a plan for you that you don't believe is possible.

It takes faith to walk in the impossible. I had to reflect back on the times that I had to use reading for my job, and the Holy Spirit showed up for me. You see, I was a preschool and kindergarten teacher in my early twenties, and I had to help the children read. By this point, I had created elaborate systems for reading,

Complete Joy

mostly of which consisted of memorizing every word I knew. But as a teacher, I was asked to help the children learn to read by implementing a system they used back then called phonics, which just never computed for me, but with the help of the Holy Spirit, I was able to do the impossible somehow. I recall getting a call from a friend one day who had talked to the mother of one of my students back then, who had graduated from high school and was so excited about his accomplishment. She told my friend to let me know the good news of his graduation and that he wanted to say thank you for helping him believe in himself and push through his challenges, and for being his favorite teacher. When she described this child to me, I remembered who he was because he struggled in my class in many ways and suffered in reading and math, especially. But we made it through together, and he was able to continue on to first grade. Can I tell you, his story touched my heart with exuberant joy, because the very struggle I experienced was what the Lord used to help someone else overcome. It's just like the Father, to take the thing we hate most about ourselves and use it to be a blessing to someone else. That's why He wants us to count it all joy through our trials, because those same obstacles we had might not just be for us; we might be the answer to so many others that are coming behind us, and as we overcome and persevere, we give others permission to believe in the impossible and even do the same.

Trusting God with Our Paths

When it feels like our world is crumbling and we can't see the way forward, it's easy to forget that God is in control. Yet Proverbs 3:5-6 gently reminds us:

"Trust in the Lord with all your heart and lean not on your own understanding; in all your ways submit to him, and he will make your paths straight."

So, what does trusting God really look like? It's about believing His word when your circumstances don't match. For example, how do you trust the Father when you get a diagnosis of stage 4 cancer and everyone in your family who got cancer has died? This level of trust requires faith. The Bible says, *"Now faith is the reality of what is hoped for, the proof of what is not seen."* (Heb 11:1) Our trust has to be rooted in our Faith that God is who He says He is. That if He says something, He can be trusted, no matter what it looks like in the natural world. My trust and faith have been tested many times over the years. This particular time was one that took every ounce of my faith to stand and call out of heaven what I needed into the earth. You see, my dad had to be taken into emergency surgery when we were at a well-known medical center in Texas to see if they could find a cure for him. While there, my dad developed a rupture in his intestines, and bile had begun to spill out into his body; if they didn't go in and close the opening, he would become septic and die. The chances of a successful surgery were not good because of the situation and his already compromised immune system, not to mention his lungs were not at full capacity; in fact, one nurse mentioned that it was the worst case of pneumonia she had ever seen. I would later learn that it wasn't pneumonia after all, because we all went into lockdown several months later due to being exposed to COVID-19. In addition, my uncle Winston had lost his battle with pneumonia several years earlier, which I know challenged my dad's faith quite a bit. The one thing you need to mix with our faith is hope, and my dad's faith was tested with the loss of his brother lost lingering in his mind as he fought for his own life. Fast forward to the surgery, and the doctors asked him to lift his DNR status because they told him this surgery was serious, and they recommended he shouldn't have that in case they needed to resuscitate. The surgery lasted several hours, and I saw a vision where my father had died and was looking down at me and my Aunt, who were in the waiting room. I began to cry out to the Lord like never before. I told him to have mercy on me, that I would not be able to handle losing my father, if he could please bring him back and give me more time to be with him. My dad was my favorite person on the planet at that time. We had just survived a challenging situation as we partnered together to take care of my stepmom, who had been sick and recently passed away. The love he showed my stepmom as she struggled to live with early-onset dementia was something out of the movies, like the movie "The Notebook" but more intense, because I witnessed this type of love first-hand, and so unconditional, may we all have someone on earth love us so well. The hours waiting and pacing the halls at the hospital went by so slowly, it felt like weeks, and I could barely open my eyes from crying so much. Then came the call for us to hear the results from the doctor, my heart had to of skipped a beat, I know I was holding my breath. With tears still being released from my eyes that I could not control, we walked into the little conference room, and the doctor who performed the surgery began to speak. What the doctor said is all a blur; I just recall it sounding like the parents of "Charlie Brown," the cartoon character I used to watch growing up… whenever they spoke on the cartoon was never audible. I remember bracing myself against the back seat of the chair I was sitting in, just in case I lost consciousness if the dreaded words of my vision were to be uttered. But to my surprise, what I heard next was, "So you can go see him now, he is awake and alert!" What? Are you kidding me! Now the tears were streaming down my face even faster as I did a speed walk to find him in his room, with the doctor and my aunt trying to keep pace with my stride. All I could do was praise God all the way there to the room, thank you Jesus, thank you Jesus, thank you so much for more time, thank you for hearing my hearts cry, thank you for answering me this way, you are so good, you are so kind, you are so faithful, how can I ever thank you enough. My heart was leaping with JOY! So much joy! When the Lord blesses you like this, it's hard to describe to others the joy you feel with words. It'll leave you speechless.

I believe this is one of the miracles of my life; it's something I'll never forget. Seeing my dad that day was so amazing, it's unforgettable in fact. Seeing him so alert, able to talk and tell me he was okay, and that he loved me. It was priceless, and I surely reciprocated these feelings, doing my best not to injure him with my overwhelming hugs and kisses. Joy unspeakable is all I say; it makes me tear up even now thinking about it. Pure joy expressed from my Heavenly Father to me by answering my prayers, then extending the time with my earthly father, whom I adore. What can be better than that?

But why is that a miracle, you ask?

Well, the vision I had in the waiting room turned out to have been real. The next day, when the doctor came to check on my dad, he confirmed he hadn't expected my dad to survive through the night, and told us that my dad had to be resuscitated during the surgery…wait what? Yes, he had died during the surgery, and they brought him back. My mouth dropped open, well, kind of, because I know what I saw and believed it. That is why my prayers were so fervent…Having my dad die that day, I pleaded with the Lord, would be more than I could handle, so he granted my request and gave me more time. I praise him for his kindness.

And it's yet another example of the miracle-working power of God, on display! Hallelujah. All I know is when miracles happen, they cause joy to rise up in a person like no other.

So, jack-up things might happen in this life, but I want to share that our God is able to do abundantly above what we could ever ask or think according to the power that works in us. (Eph 3:20). God doesn't promise to give us all the answers right away, but He does promise to guide us. Even when we can't see the path clearly, we can trust that He is leading us. More often than not, the obstacles we face aren't meant to stop us but to grow us. They're part of the process that shapes us into who God has called us to be. Even when it seems like things aren't going our way, we can take heart knowing that God's plan is at work.

The Joy of Support and Community Power

Let's face it—sometimes life's challenges are too much for us to handle on our own. And guess what? That's okay. In fact, God never intended for us to go through life's difficulties alone. He has given us a support system: family, friends, fellow believers, mentors, and even professionals who can stand with us. Galatians 6:2 calls us to:

"Carry each other's burdens, and in this way, you will fulfill the law of Christ."

Having a supportive community around us doesn't make us weak—it makes us wise. We were created for connection, and sometimes the strongest thing we can do is reach out for help when we're struggling. Whether it's a family member, trusted friend, a pastor, or a professional counselor, sharing our burdens with others lightens the load and reminds us that we don't have to carry the weight of the world on our shoulders. Asking for help can be so humbling, especially in a culture that tells us we must be strong and handle things on our own. However, this couldn't be further from the truth. Over the years, I have found that asking for help is not only wise, but it takes strength and courage, not weakness, to ask for help when we need it. Trusting those around us to carry some of our burdens can renew us and allow us to go further so we do not end up so stressed that we injure ourselves through high blood pressure, stroke, or other kinds of sickness. Because our bodies were never designed to handle prolonged stress. When my dad and stepmom found out that she had been diagnosed with earlier-onset dementia, I'm sure they had a million questions. I remember when they told me the news, my heart sank. When I went into prayer for them, the Lord said, "I'm going to send you to assist them through this journey. In fact, I'm sending you soon to assist your dad, stepmom, and your mom. I would later come to understand that the word 'assist' would be translated as helping them transition into heaven. But, praise God for not giving me all those details upfront because I would have declined that offer.

As my dad and I cared for my stepmom, Renee, God gave me some amazing restorative time with my dad. I say restorative, because Renee wasn't as fond of my relationship with my dad as I was. Being a daddy's girl ended abruptly when they got married. So, some hard choices had to be made, in my twenties, on when and how I would interact with them to save the peace for my dad and ultimately myself.

It's funny how the Lord does things. Having to go and serve unconditionally the very person who despises and does not like you doesn't exactly sound like a good plan, in my book. But that is when we really find out who we are in Christ! Can we love our enemies to the point of being their caregiver, if God called us to? Can you aid them to get where they need to go when they're blind and can't see any longer, and do it with kindness, after they just cussed you out because of the disease of dementia? Will you treat them kindly and with respect at all times, no matter what they do? The very person who caused you pain in the past, can you feed them because they can't feed themselves? Can you help them with their bathroom needs as a caregiver and show them honor and respect in this vulnerable place? Can you bless them with the love and actions of Christ working through you? These were the questions I was confronted with each day, for the 3 ½ years I lived and assisted my dad. As we both cared for and served Renee in love. I mentioned earlier that watching my dad love his wife was like witnessing a scene from the movie "The Notebook," only better. Because I vividly remember his kindness and care for her everyday. He would get up each morning, pick out her outfits, and help her get dressed so gently in the mornings.

How he would guide her to the sink and help her wash her face and brush her teeth, then take her hairbrush, brushing her hair into just the right style, she would have preferred.

Once done, with arms linked together like a chain link, they would stroll into the kitchen to the table as he prepared her breakfast, and then proceed to feed her, because she was blinded from the type of dementia she had, which made it impossible for her to see the food on the plate in front of her to feed herself. He would take her on walks, and they would sit in their car listening to her favorite music so she could sing along, while watching the sunset (although she couldn't see the beach). It was a date, nevertheless, as they sat in the car just a few blocks away from the house. These memories still touch my soul so deeply.

My love for my father led me to help him in his time of need. But can I tell you, Jesus met me in my personal mess and loved me in amazing ways by transforming my heart in so many ways during that time of serving my mom. Looking back, I can say it was such an honor to serve her in her greatest need, and I'm so humbled and blessed to have been called to be the one the Lord chose to help her. I wouldn't change this experience for anything now. May everyone get an opportunity to see Jesus's love for us in this manner, and may he work through all of us, for His glory!

Don't Forget Self-Care

In the hustle and bustle of life, it's easy to neglect ourselves. But taking time for self-care is crucial. Jesus Himself took time to rest and recharge, often retreating to quiet places to pray and reflect. If it was important for Jesus, how much more so for us? After all, He was God in the flesh, and we're just... well, mere mortals! Taking a break to do something that brings us joy— whether it's reading a book, going for a walk, or spending time with loved ones—can be incredibly refreshing.

This isn't just about indulging ourselves. Self-care helps us maintain the physical, mental, and emotional stamina we need to face life's challenges. We live in a world that glorifies busyness, but constant striving without rest can be detrimental. Taking care of ourselves, especially in times of stress, equips us to manage the obstacles and trials that we will eventually endure.

Here are a few ways you can practice self-care:

PHYSICALLY

*Getting enough Sleep — quality sleep of (7-9) hours is not only beneficial but can aid in a more joyful life.
*Move our body — Our bodies were made to move and be in motion. Try walking, dancing, stretching, biking, whatever sparks joy in you, do that.

*Eating nourishing foods — Food gives us energy, and energy brings more joy.

*Hydration — Water is essential to life, both natural and the living water that Jesus provides.

*Break Time — It's okay to step away from your screen from time to time. Schedule screen time breaks if you must to experience more joy.

MENTAL & EMOTIONAL

*Set boundaries — It's a skill we must learn, the art of saying "NO" without guilt if we want to live with joy.

*Journal — Keeping a gratitude journal can transform our lives and alleviate stress.

*Talk to someone — We all need a sounding board to process our emotions, whether it be a friend, mentor, or therapist, we don't have to struggle alone.

*Limit social media — Cutting the digital noise can lead to more peace and joy in our lives. It stops the comparison game in its tracks.

*Celebrate wins — Take time to see what you're doing well and how much you have accomplished; it's okay to breathe.

CREATIVE & RESTORATIVE

*Create something — Try something new like painting, writing, cooking, singing, let yourself explore and express yourself through art and other creative ways.

*Spend time in nature — Take a walk by the lake or hike through the mountains to refresh your soul.

*Unplug for a day — Take a digital detox, yes, it is possible and liberating!

*Pamper yourself — Yep, it's okay to do something nice for yourself once in a while. Joy is sure to return.

SPIRITUAL

*Prayer and meditation — Daily spending time in the presence of the Lord, where true joy exists.

*Read Scripture — Renewing our minds with the truth of the word. Transforms us and releases a life full of joy.

*Fellowship — Spend time with other believers to stay sharp in the spirit and fight the good fight of faith.

*Worship — Keeping Jesus at the center of our lives through worship is the key to more joy.

Hopefully, these suggestions will help us take a moment to appreciate that we can and should care for ourselves in healthy ways so we can be more joyful people. Self-care is not about being selfish, but rather it equips us to be strengthened and fortified for when the Lord may have need for us to assist others. When we are strong, we're able to release that strength to others and pull them up. Joy and strength work hand and hand.

Celebrating Small Wins

Sometimes, the challenges we face feel overwhelming because we focus solely on the big picture and forget to celebrate the small victories along the way. Philippians 1:6 encourages us:

"Being confident of this, that he who began a good work in you will carry it on to completion until the day of Christ Jesus."

Isn't it encouraging to know that Jesus is cheering us on? Not only that, but there is also a great cloud of witnesses in heaven rooting for us as we run the race of life. God isn't finished with us yet! Every little step forward, every minor victory, is a sign that God is at work, moving us closer to the fulfillment of His plan.

Sometimes, the small victories are the most powerful reminders of God's faithfulness.

A Great Cloud of Witnesses

Imagine a cheering squad in heaven, clapping and shouting every time you overcome an obstacle. Hebrews 12:1 talks about a "great cloud of witnesses" who are watching our journey with excitement, rooting for us to persevere. Knowing that we have such an audience helps remind us that we're never truly alone in our struggles. And Jesus, our greatest cheerleader, will never give up on us.

Keeping Joy Alive in the Chaos

As we push through life's obstacles, it's crucial to remember that joy isn't dependent upon circumstances, but it's a part of the fruit that's being developed in and through our lives. (Galatians 5:22-23) and it's something we can choose to cultivate, even in difficult times. Our perspective on challenges matters. Instead of allowing them to rob us of our joy, we can view them as opportunities for growth, knowing that God is with us every step of the way.

When we keep our focus on Jesus, trusting Him as our friend and helper, there's no trial we aren't equipped to handle. With God on our side, nothing is too great to overcome. Remember, the same power that raised Christ from the dead lives in us (Romans 8:11). So, why shouldn't we expect miracles in our lives? Whether those miracles happen externally or internally, through

Complete Joy

the bubbling up of joy in our hearts, God is faithful. The challenges may come, but they don't have the final word. Joy does.

Let's embrace this truth: in the face of chaos, we can experience joy that defies circumstances. When we rest in the goodness of our Father, no obstacle is too great, and no challenge can steal the joy that comes from walking with Him.

JOY NUGGET

Having true and **complete joy** doesn't mean you won't face trials or challenges; it's about trusting in the one who created you to overcome and remembering you are more than a conqueror in Christ Jesus who is the author and finisher of our faith. It's **remembering there's a fourth man in the fire with you,** like the Hebrew boys…Shadrach, Meshack, and Abednego. (Dan 3) Trust and believe **you are never alone!**

DRAWING CLOSER

Since we already know that obstacles are going to come, let us be those who prepare our hearts in advance to overcome them, knowing that it's our opportunity to lean into the strength we have in Jesus to endure. Knowing in advance that pure joy is produced in our perseverance and testing of our faith. In what way can you trust in Jesus more this week?

Scripture Reading (James 1)

Let's Pray:

Heavenly Father,

Thank You for loving us and helping us to trust in You with all our hearts, knowing that You are creating a path for us to walk that surpasses our understanding. As we acknowledge You, we realize that we are able to mount up with wings like eagles and soar above all challenges with You by our side. In the end, this refining process is necessary for us to accomplish all that You have for us in this life, bringing You glory and drawing others to know Your greatness. We surrender to Your refining fire, trusting the process and knowing that You only have good things in store for us. Let Your perfect will perfect us, in Jesus' mighty name.

Amen.

> *A joyful **HEART** is **GOOD** medicine, but a broken spirit dries up the bones.*
>
> Proverbs 17:22 (CSB)

Reflection & Revelation to Remember

CHAPTER 5

A Joyful & Grateful Heart

How Gratitude Fuels Joy

Gratitude is a simple yet powerful gift given by the Holy Spirit, one that has the capacity to revolutionize our hearts and minds. Let's dig a little deeper into the concept of gratitude to understand its profound influence on living a life full of joy. The essence of a grateful heart is deeply rooted in faith, and when we allow it to flourish, it becomes a fountain of joy, peace, and strength. As we navigate life with a spirit of peace, even amidst its many trials, by recognizing God's perfect plan for our lives, we can unlock an inner joy that cannot be diminished by the challenges we face. In this chapter, I'd like to explore how a grateful heart fuels more joy and provide insights into how joy can become a source of strength, particularly in times of adversity. Along the way, we'll examine scriptures that illustrate the divine relationship between gratitude, joy, and the peace that surpasses all understanding.

Reflection & Revelation to Remember

CHAPTER 5

A Joyful & Grateful Heart

How Gratitude Fuels Joy

Gratitude is a simple yet powerful gift given by the Holy Spirit, one that has the capacity to revolutionize our hearts and minds. Let's dig a little deeper into the concept of gratitude to understand its profound influence on living a life full of joy. The essence of a grateful heart is deeply rooted in faith, and when we allow it to flourish, it becomes a fountain of joy, peace, and strength. As we navigate life with a spirit of peace, even amidst its many trials, by recognizing God's perfect plan for our lives, we can unlock an inner joy that cannot be diminished by the challenges we face. In this chapter, I'd like to explore how a grateful heart fuels more joy and provide insights into how joy can become a source of strength, particularly in times of adversity. Along the way, we'll examine scriptures that illustrate the divine relationship between gratitude, joy, and the peace that surpasses all understanding.

A Heart of Gratitude is a Heart of Peace

When we fully surrender to the plans and will of the Father, our hearts naturally swell with gratitude and joy.

It's not difficult to find joy when we consider that the Creator of the universe, the One who made everything, has a perfect plan for each of our lives. Even better, He wants to walk with us through life, guiding us and helping us fulfill that divine plan. This thought alone should fill us with profound gratitude and joy. The Apostle Paul captured this beautifully in his letter to the Colossians when he wrote:

"Let the peace of Christ rule in your hearts, since as members of one body you were called to peace. And be thankful" (Colossians 3:15, NIV).

This verse highlights the harmonious relationship between peace and gratitude. When Christ's peace rules in our hearts, we become less anxious and less inclined to focus on what we lack or fear. Instead, we can concentrate on the blessings we've already received. Notice the second part of the verse: "And be thankful." Gratitude is the key that unlocks this peace.

One of the most beautiful byproducts of gratitude is peace. In a world where people are increasingly divisive and self-centered, the peace that comes from a grateful heart sets us apart as children of God. Jesus calls us to be peacemakers, as He mentioned in Matthew 5:9, and to love others as He has loved us. When we focus on gratitude and peace, it becomes much easier to extend grace and forgiveness to others, which is essential for walking in love and maintaining peace.

With a grateful heart, we can forgive as we have been forgiven and won't easily fall into the trap of bitterness or offense.

Let's face it: holding on to grudges or taking offense is exhausting—like carrying a backpack full of rocks uphill. But gratitude lightens the load! Think about it—if you've ever been angry at someone and then had a moment of realizing how much God has forgiven you, doesn't that make it easier to let go?

I'm recalling a time I was so angry at my mother for several years for telling a complete fabrication with all its creativity, about me, to my stepfather. She chose to become a business partner of mine, in my Mary Kay business at that time, and ran up a credit card bill that he found out about, which she had not shared she was using. Instead, she decided to lie and say I had gotten their information and purchased the items without her knowledge. Then pleaded and manipulated me not to tell him the truth because it would be the cause of her divorce. Her one lie turned into many lies, and it snowballed into an avalanche of lies, with my stepdad growing so resentful towards me that I wasn't even allowed to see my mother and could barely talk with her on the phone without confusion. Oh, and did I mention that a police report for forgery was filed against me because he believed this lie, of course, there was no truth to it, so the charges were dropped, thank God. But the lie was so solidified in my stepdad's mind that he wouldn't receive the truth. So, anytime I was around them and this subject came up, he would become angry all over again. I tried my best to make it clear that it wasn't what he thought, but nothing worked. I even found out many years later that my real father was told about this lie as well by my mother, wait…what? Why would she do that? I still don't know, because I refused to open that can of worms again, so I had to move on. It turns out that one little lie reached far and wide without my knowledge, affecting my character. I remembered being justified in my anger towards my mother for so long. Yes, I honored and respected her for being my mother, but this type of betrayal is not that easy to just let go of. Then it happened, the day the Lord confronted me with my own sin and how I was no better than my mother, whom I was holding hostage for her offense towards me. He started reminding me of all the stuff I had done that brought pain to others, even my own children, whom I loved so deeply. He said, "Do you remember the words you spoke out of anger over your son?" Do you remember the child you didn't want because it was inconvenient? Do you remember all the people and things you put ahead of me in idolatry throughout the years? Do you remember all the lies you told by trying to be someone you were not to impress others? Do you remember how making money was more important than trusting me to meet your needs? Do you remember how you needed to have a relationship to feel whole? It just kept coming, one thing after another, until I was like, okay, okay, I've had enough. Please forgive me, Lord, please forgive me. That's when the Holy Spirit spoke to me so gently in that pain and said I already have, you are forgiven for all of it, the day you accepted Jesus! And I've forgiven your mother, too. The pain she caused you is real, and I know it hurt you, but she is my daughter as well, and her cries have come up to me just as yours have. I am a merciful father who cares about and loves all of my children.

What I do for one, I can do for another, whether you agree with my choices or not. I am just in my renderings, and you will have to trust me to vindicate you for the wrongs done towards you.

You'll have to trust me to handle all that has transpired. Nothing goes unnoticed. Forgive your mom, as I have forgiven you. Not so she can go free, but ... so you can!

And just like that, a flood of emotions, both good and bad, turned into a sense of peace and gratitude. A renewed hope came over me. I felt something lift off of me that day. I still had to deal with the residue every now and then from time to time, but as I kept saying, "I have forgiven you for that offense," it eventually became real in my mind and heart, until one day the sting of it all was gone. Gratitude, along with forgiveness, can diffuse even the most intense emotions. And if you're too busy counting your blessings, you're less likely to keep score of offenses.

The peace and joy that flow from this kind of heart are contagious. It doesn't just affect your own spirit but also extend to those around you. It's like a spiritual ripple effect. Just imagine walking through your day with a heart full of peace, joy, and gratitude. You'll naturally radiate more love and effectively release it to others. Proverbs 17:22 says:

"A cheerful heart is good medicine, but a crushed spirit dries up the bones.".

A grateful heart is a heart full of joy, and that joy is contagious, offering healing and renewal to those we encounter. It's good medicine not just for us, but for everyone we meet!

The Role of Gratitude in Trials

Now, you might be wondering, "What about when life gets hard? How can I be grateful when I'm going through trials?" We touched on this earlier, and the truth is that's a valid question. No one enjoys difficult times, but the Bible makes it clear that trials are not pointless. In fact, they are opportunities for growth, and—believe it or not—for joy. James 1:2-3 tells us:

"Consider it pure joy, my brothers and sisters, whenever you face trials of many kinds, because you know that the testing of your faith produces perseverance."

Wait a second—joy in trials? Is James serious? Yes, he is! James isn't suggesting that we should be happy about our trials in the sense that we enjoy suffering. Instead, he's pointing out that trials are a chance to grow, to trust God more deeply, and to experience the joy of His presence and provision in the midst of difficulty.

One of the most valuable lessons we can learn is to trust God in the midst of trials.

We have several examples in the Bible that highlight this ability to trust in God's plans over our own.

Remember the story in chapter 3 in the book of Daniel.

Here we find Shadrach, Meshach, and Abednego, three Hebrew boys who decided they were not going to follow the king Nebuchadnezzar's decrees. But instead, they would follow the laws of the Most High God of Israel and not bow down to any golden image, no matter who gave the orders. This infuriated King Nebuchadnezzar and he ordered that they be punished by death in the fiery furnace. He ordered his men to turn the fire up 7 times hotter, but as they were carrying the boys up to get into the fire, the king's men were burned up, due to the intense heat. The boys were placed in the fire, when all of a sudden, the king jumped up in alarm. *He asks his advisers, "Did we not throw three men, bound, into the fire?" Yes, of course, your majesty," they replied to the king. He exclaimed, "Look! I see four men, not tied, walking around in the fire unharmed; and the fourth looks like a son of the gods." Nebuchadnezzar then approached the door of the furnace of blazing fire and called, "Shadrach, Meshach, and Abednego, you servants of the Most High God, come out!" So Shadrach, Meshach, and Abednego came out of the fire.* (Dan 3:24-26).

When they examined the boys, their bodies were not burned, their hair was all in place, and they didn't even smell like smoke.

Nebuchadnezzar gave praise to the God of Israel and issued a decree that no one should say anything offensive about the God of the 3 Hebrew boys, or they would be torn limb from limb and their houses would be destroyed. He then proclaimed, "Because there is no other God who is able to deliver like this!" Then he rewarded them. Wow, now how about that for going through a trial and coming out the other side more victorious than you went in? Hallelujah!

It's not easy, but when we finally come through our trials, we find that joy doesn't come from the absence of problems, but from knowing that God is with us through them. The peace and joy that we gain from trusting God are priceless. In John 16:33, Jesus told His disciples:

"In this world, you will have trouble. But take heart! I have overcome the world."

Jesus never promised us a problem-free life, but He did promise us His presence and His victory. When we remember that Jesus has already overcome the world, we can face our own trials with confidence and gratitude. It's like knowing the end of a movie before it starts—you don't have to worry because you know how it turns out. Our trials may be tough, but they don't last forever, and they don't define us. What defines us is our relationship with God, our ability to trust Him, and our willingness to persevere with gratitude, even when things get tough.

Now, let's talk about perseverance. I don't know about you, but for me, perseverance sometimes feels like trying to finish a marathon with no finish line in sight. It's easy to get discouraged. That's why having a grateful heart is so important. Gratitude shifts our focus from what's wrong to what's right. It reminds us of God's faithfulness in the past and assures us that He will be faithful in the future. And as we persevere, trusting God through the ups and downs, our faith grows stronger, and so does our joy.

In fact, the more we persevere, the more joy we'll experience, because Joy isn't just about what's happening around us. It's about what's happening inside of us. As we walk through trials with gratitude, trusting God every step of the way, we become more resilient, more peaceful, and yes, more joyful. The trials we face today prepare us for the victories we'll experience tomorrow.

Joy in Obedience and Surrender

Let's take a moment to talk about obedience. Because, let's be honest, sometimes God will ask us to do things that we really don't want to do. I'm sure you've been there— I know I have. It's like God says, "I have a wonderful plan for your life," and you're thinking, "Great! What is it?" And then He asks you to do something that feels, well, impossible—or at least highly inconvenient.

Let me give you an mild example from my own life. I remember the time I had just gone on a glorious shopping spree. Everything I bought fit perfectly... (which, for a tall person like me, is no small miracle).

I was so excited to wear my new outfits, and I was already planning which one I'd wear first. Then, just as I got home, I felt the Lord prompting me to give all of the outfits to my neighbor. Wait—what? No, that can't be right. Surely, I misheard Him. But no, the Lord made it clear. He wanted me to give my brand-new clothes to my neighbor.

I wish I could tell you that I immediately obeyed with a joyful heart, but that's not exactly how it went. I wrestled with it for a while. I even tried on the clothes again, just to be sure they were as perfect as I thought they were. But the Lord was persistent, and eventually, I surrendered. I took the clothes to my neighbor, and as much as I wanted her to refuse them, she accepted them gratefully.

A few weeks later, I saw her wearing one of the outfits, and it fit her perfectly. Seeing her joy brought me a kind of happiness I hadn't expected. In that moment, I realized that obedience, even when it's difficult, brings a deeper kind of joy than anything else. There's something about doing what God asks, even when it's hard, that fills your heart with a sense of purpose and fulfillment.

Jesus understood this well. In John 15:10-11, He said:

"If you keep my commands, you will remain in my love, just as I have kept my Father's commands and remain in His love. I have told you this so that my joy may be in you and that your joy may be complete."

Obedience leads to complete joy. Why? Because when we obey the Father, we prove that we love him. If we want to have that real and lasting joy fully in our lives, we must obey whatever the Lord asks of us. What is obedience? It's compliance or submission to authority. When we obey God, even in the little things, we experience the fullness of His joy. Today's culture will tell you it's not necessary to submit to authority, do whatever you want. But we serve a God of order, and his kingdom is run differently from the world; it's the complete opposite. Submission is not a bad word or means you are lesser than; it actually takes great strength to submit with the right heart posture. We all have our own ideas of how things should be or run, so when we allow someone to take that position in our life over us, it requires humility. Humility is strength under control. Our greatest example of submission is Jesus, who submitted to endure the cross and allowed himself to be arrested by the high priest for a crime he did not commit. He had the ability and choice to call down 12 legions of angels to his defense, but he submitted to the Father's will and went to the cross for us all. Our greatest advocate and king denied his own desires and laid down his life in obedience to show us and save us from our sins. Obedience and submission are actually an honor and a privilege we are allowed to partake in, and the results lead to amazing joy in our lives. Now that sounds crazy to the world we live in. It's flipped upside down, completely. There's another part—obedience is like a muscle. The more we practice it, the stronger it gets. The more we surrender to God's will, the easier it becomes to trust Him, and the more joy we'll experience.

Gratitude in Worship

Have you noticed how both gratitude and worship keep coming up in this book repeatedly? It's because they are keys to living in a place of complete joy, and it's fueled by our obedience.

If you're looking for a practical way to cultivate a grateful heart, I have one word for you: worship. Worship is a powerful way to express gratitude and remind ourselves of God's goodness. The Psalms are full of calls to worship and give thanks. For example, Psalm 100:4 says:

"Enter His gates with thanksgiving and His courts with praise; give thanks to Him and praise His name."

When we worship, we are reminded of who God is and what He has done. Worship shifts our focus from our problems to God's greatness.

Worship doesn't have to be complicated. It can be as simple as turning on some worship music and singing along or taking a few minutes each day to thank God for His blessings. I've found that when I start my day with worship, everything else falls into place. It's like tuning my heart to the right frequency. Worship helps me focus on what matters most—God's love, His faithfulness, and His presence in my life.

Ephesians 5:19-20 encourages us to:

"Speak to one another with psalms, hymns, and songs from the Spirit. Sing and make music from your heart to the Lord, always giving thanks to God the Father for everything, in the name of our Lord Jesus Christ."

Giving thanks to God through worship is a beautiful way to connect with God and experience Him. As we worship, we enter God's presence, and miraculous things happen in the presence of God. We experience healing for our souls, renewed strength when we're weary, restored hope for the future, and the power to endure tough times. This is a time and place to make our request known to our Father, who wants us to come to him unafraid and in boldness to seek him for directions for our lives and to ask him for what we need. It's also a time we can share our hearts with him about those we love and care about. Where can we release our concerns about the world around us that's in upheaval and tumultuous? As the days ahead keep getting dark, learning to find a special time and space to be with the Father in worship is going to be more needed than ever. Now is the time we should get into the habit of listening to what's on his heart and learning to pray and worship from that place. He has given us the ability to bring what He wants into the earth through our prayers and petitions. It's an amazing feeling knowing that your prayers, worship, and heart posture allow us to have our requests heard and answered. That we can help to shift something on the earth that God wanted to happen. He wants us to say what he says, so he can release his angels to bring it to pass. How much more joy would you experience each day if you knew your requests were being heard in the courts of heaven and initiated in the earth because you spent time with the Lord in worship and prayer? We shouldn't take our times of worship for granted; true worship changes things here on earth for the better.

The Joy of the Lord is Your Strength

Perhaps one of the most well-known verses about joy is found in (Nehemiah 8:10): *"The joy of the Lord is your strength."*

This verse is a powerful reminder that joy isn't just a pleasant feeling—it's a source of strength. When we are joyful, we have more resilience to handle stressful situations and conflicts because joy acts like a buffer. Our responses are filled with grace and kindness instead of fear. When we cultivate joy, it comes from a place of knowing God; this joy gives us the strength to face whatever life throws our way.

Joy rooted in the Father is a powerful force. It doesn't depend on our circumstances but on our relationship with God. When we choose to focus on His goodness, trust His plan, and express our gratitude through worship, we tap into a joy that cannot be shaken. And

Complete Joy

that joy gives us the strength to persevere, to love others, and to live a life that reflects God's glory.

Some practical ways to incorporate joy in your life, as your strength, might be:

*Remember how laughter and joy can shift the room and change the atmosphere in your day. It can be a burst of hope and energy to help you through the day.

*Joy can boost your faith and hope. Believing the Lord is with you in every circumstance will give you the faith to press through.

*Fear and doubt can drain our strength. But joy works like a force field shielding us from the fiery darts of the enemy that try to bombard our thoughts, but you can't think joyful and fearful thoughts at the same time. Joy helps to shift your focus to what is right and helps you leave what's wrong behind.

*Joy can alleviate stress and boost your immune system. It's literally like a medicine, so take your Joy vitamins every day.

*Joy is contagious. Walking in joy uplifts those around you and builds stronger unity in your community.

So, as you go through your day, take a moment to reflect on the ways God has blessed you. How can you be a conduit for joy to those in your sphere of influence? Let His joy fuel you. Let joy be your strength. Whether you're facing trials, walking in obedience, or simply going about your daily routine, remember that a joyful heart is the key to experiencing the fullness of God has for you.

In the end, it's about aligning our hearts with God's, trusting His plan, and living in a way that reflects His love and goodness to the world around us. And when we do that, we'll find that joy is not something we have to chase—it's something that overflows naturally.

JOY NUGGET

Gratitude shifts our focus from what's missing to the miraculous, **turning what we already have into more than enough.** In that place, you'll find contentment laced with joy.

DRAWING CLOSER

Gratitude is how we recognize and train our hearts that God is working out every aspect of our lives, and He can be trusted. It deepens our intimacy with the Father; the more

thankful we are, the more we see His goodness all around us. Allowing pure joy to flow in and through our lives.

Scripture Reading (Luke 17)

Let's Pray:

Heavenly Father,

We are so grateful for Your goodness and the love You continue to pour over our lives each day. Even in the midst of trials, You are still with us, guiding and directing us into Your perfect will and producing the endurance we need to carry out Your plan. We thank You for releasing more strength in us through joy and for helping us acknowledge You in all things, even when things are hard. Thank You for the peace and joy You give us each day as we walk and trust in You.

Amen.

> *I have told you these things so that my **JOY** may be in you and your joy may be **COMPLETE**.*
>
> John 15:11 (CSB)

Reflection & Revelation to Remember

CHAPTER 6

Joyful Relationships

Connecting Through Joy

Relationships—ah, the joy they bring when they're going well! But if you've been on this planet for any length of time, I don't need to tell you that people can do strange "people things" that make life sour, like lemons. Yet, instead of trying to win every battle, we must remember that compromise works much better for keeping joy and peace in our lives. It's in these trying times that we need the joy of the Lord to be our compass and anchor, helping us stay calm and push through the storms. Because we know, "The joy of the Lord is our strength." We know joy gives us the strength to navigate the ups and downs of relationships with grace and peace.

What's amazing is how the Lord uses our relationships to reveal things about ourselves that He wants to change. Have you ever been in a situation where you're praying for God to fix the other person—your spouse, your child, your friend—and then suddenly you realize, "Wait a minute... maybe I'm the problem?" Jesus spoke about this in Matthew 7:3, when He asked why we look at the speck in our brother's eye while ignoring the plank in our own. I've experienced this revelation more times than I care to admit, and it's humbling. It can even steal our joy for a while. But here's the silver lining: when we surrender to God and allow Him to work on us, our relationships are restored, and with them, our joy.

Humility in Relationships: A Path to Joy

Philippians 2:3-4 urges us: *"Do nothing out of selfish ambition or vain conceit. Rather, in humility, value others above yourselves, not looking to your own interests but each of you to the interests of others."* The Lord calls us to walk in humility, and let me tell you, in today's "me-first" culture, that's no easy feat! But humility is the key to joy. You see, thinking of others before ourselves not only reflects Christ's love, but it can also deepen our relationships and create more intimacy. Having the freedom to be authentically who we are around others, especially our spouse and loved ones, allows a sense of freedom. As we live our lives in this freedom will find that we are living in complete joy.

Now, let's not misunderstand this. Walking in humility doesn't mean becoming a doormat or never addressing real issues. It means recognizing that we're all works in progress. We are a masterpiece, designed to do good works that our Heavenly Father designed for us before we even came to the earth. (2 Corn 5:17) Knowing this about ourselves and others allows us to give grace where grace is needed. When we make others feel valued and prioritize their needs over our own, something beautiful happens—joy. True, unshakable joy.

In a world where self-centeredness reigns, we often feel lonely and empty. It's a paradox, really. The more we focus on ourselves, the more isolated we become. God created us for connection, for relationship. Ecclesiastes 4:9-10 tells us: *"Two are better than one, because they have a good return for their labor: If either of them falls down, one can help the other up."* When we invest in relationships and serve others, we step into the divine design for our lives, and with it comes joy.

What does humility look like in our relationships, and how can we implement it practically?

1. Listening before speaking —humble people seek to understand and are good listeners, they value the opinions of others, and don't need to dominate a conversation.

2. Admitting our wrongs—humility acknowledges our own imperfections and allows us to say "I was wrong" without excuses or being defensive.

3. A heart that's quick to forgive—Humility doesn't keep records of wrong or hold grudges, remembering how much forgiveness has been given to them.

4. Can serve without credit—Humility can serve quietly, without applause or recognition.

5. Humility doesn't have to be right, but prioritizes unity, for the sake of keeping the peace and loving others.

6. Can celebrate without comparison—and is genuinely happy for other successes.

7. Humility can receive correction well, and doesn't become offended, but has a teachable heart posture.

8. Values others—walking in love and really valuing the uniqueness and design of another one of God's creations.

With these values in mind, we can begin to implement them over time by creating new habits and being intentional about staying humble. Asking God to reveal and search our hearts for things He wants to remove or adjust. We can be the first to apologize when a dispute arises, work to ask more questions and really be interested in others' lives around us, serve others quietly, and pray for others without them having to know. Learning to embrace correction and not rush to defend ourselves. We also want to speak well of others publicly and privately, and especially encourage them directly. And most importantly, we want to meditate on Jesus and how he walked in humility. He is our ultimate example of humility, even enduring the cross. He is our model of strength under control, where real humility comes from. (Phil 2:5-8) Our relationships will be enriched as we walk in humility, and joy will flow like a river in our lives.

Vulnerability: The Gateway to Deep Connection and Joy

Being vulnerable in relationships can be hard. Opening up and allowing someone to see the real us takes courage because the more we reveal, the more someone can hurt us. Yet, vulnerability is the key to forming meaningful, joy-filled relationships. Proverbs 27:6 says: *"Faithful are the wounds of a friend; profuse are the kisses of an enemy."* This means that even when our friends hurt us (hopefully unintentionally), there is potential for deeper growth and intimacy on the other side of that pain. Because these wounds are coming from a place of loving redirection or correction, honest feedback, or truth spoken in love—even if it hurts initially. You're blessed if you find a true friend like this, because true friends care more about your well-being than your comfort. They will protect you from doing something destructive and will confront you. This will hopefully protect you and help you grow. These types of "wounds" are acts of love, not betrayal, meant to heal and not harm. So, the next time a friend points out pride, laziness, or hidden sin, thank them for being loving enough to tell you the truth.

But vulnerability can be risky. When people repeatedly disappoint us, it's tempting to shut down. However, trusting God with our hearts rather than relying on people to protect them opens the door to joy. Psalm 28:7 proclaims: *"The Lord is my strength and my shield; my heart trusts in him, and he helps me. My heart leaps for joy."* When we put our trust in God, we release the pressure on others to be perfect, and we find joy because our security rests in Him. The Father can always be trusted.

We all know the sad reality that we have all hurt someone, intentionally or not. That's why we need God's grace to love others as we should. When we're honest about our shortcomings, it not only builds trust but deepens our relationships. There's something about sharing our imperfections that allows others to connect with us on a more human level. James 5:16 says: *"Therefore, confess your sins to each other and pray for each other so that you may be healed."* Vulnerability and honesty in our relationships can foster emotional healing. God has a way of stepping into our pain and not only drawing us closer to Him but to one another. Being vulnerable can be a gift when we're open to allowing others to see us more deeply.

Encouragement and Prayer: Strengthening Relationships

One of the greatest joys in relationships comes from encouraging and building each other up. 1Thessalonians 5:11 says, *"Therefore encourage one another and build each other up, just as in fact you are doing."* When we encourage others, we give them the strength to keep going. Encouragement has a multiplying effect—it not only strengthens the other person but also fills our own hearts with joy.

Furthermore, when we pray for others, we invite God into the relationship. James 5:16 tells us, *"Therefore, confess your sins to one another and pray for one another, so that you may be healed. The prayer of a righteous person is very powerful in its effect."* Righteousness is not about being perfect, but having a right standing with the Father. We live in this way when we walk in humility, we are quick to repent, and we pursue God's will for our lives. It's about our heart posture to obey the Father and align our lives with his plans and purposes for us. When a righteous person prays, therefore, it has the power to move heaven and earth, not because of their powers but because of their connection to the power source and authority of God. When we can be transparent and humble before others and God, we invite his healing power into our situation. As we pray together, we strengthen each other, and healing can flow through our unity. Intercession is a powerful gift we can bestow upon other believers and can help to shift the trajectory of their lives for the better. And when those prayers are answered, oh, the joy it brings! What could bring more joy than seeing God answer prayers for those we love?

And don't forget the favor of God. Psalm 5:12 says, *"Surely, Lord, you bless the righteous; you surround them with your favor as with a shield."* Imagine walking through life with a shield of divine favor around you! This favor comes when we walk in righteousness, even in our relationships. Choosing to forgive, to bless rather than curse, and to extend grace when it's least deserved—all of these choices invite God's favor into our lives. The word "surround" is a military word that means to enclose on all sides; encompass, which means to form a circle around. Now imagine God placing a force shield all around you called favor, it's constant and encircling. A shield is a protective force against attacks, slander, failure, or harm. But it's not just defensive—it gives us confidence to move forward knowing God has our back. Favor in Hebrew means grace, goodwill, delight, kindness, or unmerited assistance. You can't earn this gift from God; it's His goodness and love for us that make it possible. It's when doors open you didn't knock on. When people help you and don't know why. It's when you succeed in places you were disqualified for on paper. Favor is an invisible advantage that changes the world around us. We can walk in God's favor by being righteous and staying humble. Declaring it over our lives and our families and having an expectation for favor to show up in our lives. Just believe and know surely the Lord will bless you with goodness and mercy and abundant favor all of your days of your life.

The Sacrifices We Make for Love

There's no getting around it: love requires sacrifice. Sometimes, God will ask us to lay certain relationships on the altar. Why? Often, it's because those relationships have become idols in our hearts. Exodus 34:14 tells us, *"Do not worship any other god, for the Lord, whose name is Jealous, is a jealous God."* Sometimes, God asks us to release relationships to Him so that He can take His rightful place in our hearts.

It can be hard to let go, especially when it's someone we deeply care about. But we must remember: God always knows what's best. When Abraham was asked to sacrifice Isaac, it was a test of his heart (Genesis 22). God asked Abraham to sacrifice his long-awaited son, which was a miracle from the start. Because he and his wife, Sarah, were incredibly old at the time, way too old to have children naturally. But they believed God and received the promise, and now God is asking him to sacrifice the very one that was promised. How can that be? These are the mysteries of God that require faith and surrender. Learning to trust that God is always faithful to His word. Abraham believed just what He was told and took Issac to be sacrificed. His own son asked him where the sacrifice was to be offered, and Abraham told him in faith, "God will provide," and sure enough, just like that, an angel appeared to stop him. Wow, now that's faith. Do you have faith like that when it comes to those you love? If God told you to give up a family member or friend, could you? Would you? When God asks us to surrender a relationship, it's often a similar test. And just as God provided a ram in place of Isaac, He will provide what we need when we trust Him.

Sometimes, after the test, He gives the relationship back, stronger and better than before. Other times, He asks us to let go entirely. Either way, our joy comes from knowing that God is in control and that He has good plans for us. We've all experienced how clinging too tightly to people can steal our joy. But when we release them to God, we find peace and joy in knowing He is sovereign over all things—including our relationships.

God's Love: The Source of Joy

Let's talk about love, specifically God's love. Our culture has really watered down the concept of love, using the same word to describe our feelings for pizza, fashion, and our closest friends. But the Bible says, *"God is love"* (1 John 4:8). His love is not just an emotion; it's His very essence. It's vast, overwhelming, indescribable, and without flaw. (Ephesians 3:17-19) *"So that Christ may dwell in your heart through faith —that you, being rooted and grounded in love, may have strength to comprehend with all the saints what is the breadth and length and height and depth, and to know the love of Christ that surpasses knowledge, that you may be filled with all the fullness of God."* It's a love that surpasses our ability to comprehend or understand with our minds alone, and even with all the information available to us today, through the internet or AI. God's love must be experienced through a real encounter; it's a gift of God that is given to those who diligently seek Him. The Bible say's *"You will seek me and find me, when you seek me with all your heart"* (Jer 29:13). Unfortunately, there are a lot of people who know about God and what He will and will not do for them, but they don't know him as a friend. Can I tell you, the Father wants to have a friendship with us. He wants to lavish His love on us and tell us secrets as we draw closer to him. He desires intimacy with us. He wants us to desire him more than anything else in this world, so He can pour out this love without measure upon us. Wow, who wouldn't want to know and serve a God so gracious?

When we experience this kind of love, God's love, it transforms us. Because the truth is, the most powerful relationship we can have and cultivate is getting to know the Father, understanding the sacrifice Jesus made for us on the cross, and how the Holy Spirit lives in and through us to help us carry out our assignments here on the earth. You are not here by accident or random chance; you were created by a creative God, who fashioned you into His image to reflect his glory in the earth, to reflect a part of His very nature. He wants to put you on display and show off who He is to others. He wants to demonstrate his love for others through your life. We have the privilege to know and love him and ultimately be used to love others with the help of the Holy Spirit through serving them with the gifts and talents we possess. When we do, the glory and love of God are put on display, and they can come to love and serve Him, too. God's plan is so brilliant and so good.

This kind of love is so deep and so wide, it's this kind of love that led Jesus to lay down His life for us (John 15:13), "Greater love has no one than this, that someone lay down his life for his friends," and it's this same sacrificial love that fills us with unshakable joy. God's love changes us in ways we could never imagine. It compels us to give, to serve, and to love others. Romans 5:5 tells us that God's love has been poured out into our hearts through the Holy Spirit, and with it comes the fruit of joy (Galatians 5:22).

Complete Joy

God's love is the only thing that truly fulfills us completely. We are born into the world with a desire and hunger that only the Father in heaven can fill. He created us to want to worship Him and then left us clues on how to find Him all around us, so no one will have an excuse to say they didn't see Him. His love is on display in nature, in the stars and galaxies above, in the oceans so deep, in the people all around us. You have to work really hard not to see Him. There's a hunger inside all of us that knows instinctively that there is something missing, too, when we don't know him or his love for us. We will search long and wide, unfortunately, trying to put something else into that void that only the Father can fill. Thank God, we serve a patient Father who waits and gives us chance after chance to find him for real; it's His loving mercies that wait for us. It's a gift we even come to know

Him. Did you know the Father has to draw you and open your eyes so you can see Him and His love for you? We can't even boast about finding Him, because He was pursuing us the whole time. Now that's real love. No relationship on earth can fill the deep need for love and acceptance that we all carry. Only God can do that. When we grasp this truth, we stop expecting others to meet needs that only God can fulfill. We stop placing unrealistic expectations on our relationships, and that, my friends, is where joy begins. I'll say it again, it's in His love, we find the fullness of joy!

Cultivating Joyful Relationships

Ultimately, our joy in relationships flows from our relationship with God. As we grow closer to Him, we are transformed into His image—an image of love. The more time we spend in His presence, the more His joy fills us, and that joy spills over into all our other relationships. 2 Corinthians 3:18 reminds us that *" we are being transformed into His image with ever-increasing glory."* When we are filled with the love of God, we love others better, and in doing so, we cultivate joy in our relationships.

The secret to more joyful relationships is simple: spend more time with the Father. Let Him fill you with His love and watch how that transforms your relationships. Let His love for you be your foundation for more meaningful, strong, and healthy relationships—ultimately brimming with joy.

JOY NUGGET

Healthy relationships with Jesus at the center are like sunlight to the soul's garden—it helps joy bloom. We weren't designed to be alone but in deep connection with one another. Our joy multiplies when it's shared.

DRAWING CLOSER

Jesus modeled how to have meaningful relationships with others. He laughed, cried with friends, served and washed the feet of his disciples, and even ate with the outcast. He didn't just teach us about joy but lived it out in community. We find real joy in sacrificial love, vulnerability, and through serving others. It's not always easy, but it's worth the effort to develop deep and lasting friendships. The type of friendship that deposits joy into our lives for years to come.

Scripture Reading (Hebrews 10)

Let's Pray:

Heavenly Father,

We thank You for the joy that comes from our relationships. Thank You for being a relational God, and for the promise that as we develop our relationship and friendship with You, we will have more joyful and fulfilling relationships with others. Help us to be more gracious to those around us, so that joy becomes a byproduct and expression of Your love.

We ask for an increase in joy in our lives, along with the lives of our families and friends. Amen.

> *But the **FRUIT** of the **SPIRIT** is love, joy, peace, patience, kindness, goodness, faithfulness.*
>
> Galatians 5:22 (CSB)

Reflection & Revelation to Remember

CHAPTER 7

The Essence of Joy

Understanding Our Divine Nature

The essence of joy is a divine gift that, as believers, we are all called to embrace. It is one of the attributes of the fruit of the Spirit described in Galatians 5:22-23, where the Apostle Paul writes:

"But the fruit of the Spirit is love, joy, peace, patience, kindness, goodness, faithfulness, gentleness, and self-control. Against such things there is no law."

This joyous spiritual essence in the fruit is not something we strive to produce on our own through sheer willpower. Rather, it begins to manifest in us from the moment we accept Jesus as our Lord and Savior. Like a tree bearing fruit in its season, the Holy Spirit cultivates these attributes within us as we grow closer to our Father in Heaven.

Interestingly, joy shouldn't be isolated from the other parts of the fruit. It works in harmony with the other attributes of the Spirit and is deeply intertwined with them, particularly love. Instead of viewing joy in isolation, let's explore how it is nurtured in our lives through its relationship with other attributes of the Spirit. Spoiler alert: If you're looking for a shortcut to joy, start with love.

It's Love: The Foundation of Joy

Love is the cornerstone upon which all the other elements of this fruit of the Spirit stand. Without love, the rest cannot fully flourish. As we read in 1 John 4:8, "God is love," and His love is woven into every aspect of our divine nature. It's like the glue that holds all these lovely qualities together, and without it, joy would not exist.

The Apostle Paul tells us in 1 Corinthians 13:4-7:

"Love is patient, love is kind. It does not envy, it does not boast, it is not proud. It does not dishonor others, it is not self-seeking, it is not easily angered, it keeps no record of wrongs. Love does not delight in evil but rejoices with the truth. It always protects, always trusts, always hopes, always perseveres."

Love carries so many beautiful qualities—patience, kindness, humility, forgiveness—that it naturally leads to joy. Imagine the ripple effect of these qualities in our lives: when we act in love, we align more closely with God's nature, and that alignment brings us joy. It's as if joy is love's natural by-product.

And love isn't something we reserve for grand moments, like forgiving someone for a major offense.

No, love is most powerfully expressed in the small, daily acts of kindness.

Acts of Kindness: Small Seeds, Big Harvest of Joy

Let's take a moment to think about kindness. What if the love embedded in acts of kindness was something we intentionally worked to release into the world, one act at a time? Imagine if, throughout our day and week, we were on the lookout for opportunities to be kind—moments where God gently highlights ways we could brighten someone's day. It doesn't have to be grand or life-changing, though sometimes it can be. What if it were as simple as calling an old friend you haven't spoken to in a while, just to let them know how their friendship has made your life better? Not only would this warm their heart, but it might also remind them of their value in this world—a feeling we all need from time to time.

Or picture this: spending an hour with an elderly neighbor. Perhaps they live alone and don't have many visitors, but they have a lifetime of stories just waiting to be told. You could bring a smile to their face by showing genuine interest in their experiences and the wisdom they've gathered over the years. It's funny how something so seemingly small, like taking the time to listen, can have such a profound impact and increase our joy.

And if you're feeling a bit more daring, why not take it a step further? How about the next time you're at the grocery store, secretly paying for the groceries of the single mom standing ahead of you in line? It might feel like a bit of a risk, but just imagine the relief and gratitude she'd feel in that moment.

She might have been silently praying for a break, and there you are— God's answer to her prayer, offering kindness without expecting anything in return.

The list of ways we can be kind is practically endless. Yet, so often, we miss these opportunities because we're focused on ourselves instead of tuning in to what God might be nudging us toward. It's easy to get caught up in our own little worlds—our schedules, our to-do lists, our stresses—but what if we paused and listened for those divine promptings to be kind? How might that change things, not only for the people around us but for ourselves as well?

You see, kindness doesn't just bless the recipient. Sure, it brightens their day, but there's a beautiful boomerang effect that happens with kindness. It blesses us, too. It produces a joy that wells up in both the giver and the receiver. And here's a little secret: when people are full of joy, they're not usually out there committing evil acts.

Complete Joy

Joy and malice don't coexist very well.

In fact, kindness can be contagious. Think about it—when someone shows us unexpected kindness, doesn't it inspire us to pass it on? That feeling of joy we get from being on the receiving end of kindness has this almost miraculous ability to compel us to be kind to someone else. It's like kindness multiplies. A ripple effect that expands as vast as the sea itself. And when kindness starts to spread, it becomes a force for good in a world that desperately needs it.

Kindness, at its core, is a form of love. It's one of the many expressions of love that make up the fruit of the Spirit.

When we practice being kind and loving toward others, the more we grow. It's not always easy, and sometimes it takes a conscious effort, but each small act of kindness is like watering our spiritual garden, helping our fruit to mature.

God wants us to grow in love, to represent Him to those we encounter through our actions. Real love, the kind God calls us to embody, is full of the Spirit. It doesn't think of itself or demand its own way. Real love is patient, even when people test our patience to the limit. It doesn't hold grudges or keep score. Instead, love is slow to anger, willing to give people another chance, and even willing to forget their wrongs altogether. It's the kind of love that protects, even when it's not convenient, and stands by you when you've messed up. Love doesn't get jealous when someone else is blessed with something you've been waiting for. Love is secure enough to be happy for others and trust that your time will come, too.

Real love can be trusted. It hopes for the best, even when the situation looks bleak. It sticks with you, especially when life is hard and things aren't going as planned. When you meet a person who loves like this, you're bound to notice something else about them: they radiate joy. They have an abundance of joy in their heart, and that joy spills over into every aspect of their life.

Now, I know what you're thinking—people like that are rare. And you're right. It's not every day that you meet someone who loves with such grace and selflessness. But here's the good news: we can all become that kind of person. It starts with the small, simple acts of kindness we talked about earlier. It starts with being willing to look beyond ourselves and listen to those little nudges from God to reach out and show love to someone else.

Maybe that's what the world needs more of right now. We live in a time where it seems like there's so much division, so much anger, and fear. But kindness has the power to cut through all the noise and pick up the sound of heaven. The sound of love, being released through us. This sound carries a frequency of deliverance, peace, and freedom. This sound carries our breakthrough for abundance in every area of our lives. It carries joy and brings it into the earth. It has the power to heal, to bring people together, and to remind us of our shared need to be known by God and by others.

Kindness creates unity. And unity is what our Father, Jesus, and the Holy Spirit represent to us in heaven. This is our example; we should endeavor to represent this same unity on Earth. Unity isn't about being the same; it's about being okay with our differences, but coming together under one purpose. It's about oneness in our values and beliefs towards a common goal or objective. Imagine your favorite sports team, each player has their unique skill set, but they work together to win. The Father is calling us to unite as His heavenly children on the earth through our love, truth, and mission that centers around the redemption of God's children through Jesus. It's not our goal to just get along; it's about linking arm and arms to express God's goodness to those around us in all we do.

The more we practice kindness, the more we reflect God's love to the world. And as we do that, we'll find that the joy we give to others will find its way back to us. It's a divine cycle—

God's way of showing us that in giving, we receive. We can live in harmony with one another, having one mind and one heart. Because we have the mind of Christ, the greatest mind that ever existed. Let's strive to release this love into the world, one small act of kindness at a time. Who knows? We might just start a kindness and joy movement.

Let's remember—Proverbs 11:25 says, *"A generous person will prosper; whoever refreshes others will be refreshed."* In other words, kindness not only blesses others but also brings blessings—and joy—back to us.

The Peace of God: A Fortress of Joy

Alongside love and kindness, peace is another element of the Spirit that nurtures joy. Have you ever noticed how peaceful people often carry a quiet joy with them? They're not easily shaken, and their unflappable attitude stems from a deep trust in God.

In Hebrew, the word for peace is "shalom," which means wholeness, completeness, and unity with God.

Shalom's core meaning is described as:

*Peace—calmness, harmony, and well-being.

*Wholeness—being complete or lacking nothing.

*Prosperity—thriving in every area: spiritually, emotionally, physically, and relationally.

*Health and Safety—freedom from danger, harm, or fear.

*Rest—inner stillness and balance, not just physical rest.

This is describing a peace that is complete, and it only comes from the Father. Shalom is a restoration to the way things should be in our relationship with God, ourselves, others, and creation.

In (Numbers 6:24-26)— *"The Lord bless you and keep you; the Lord make his face to shine upon you and be gracious to you; the Lord lift up his countenance upon you and give you peace (shalom)."*

Shalom is more than our English word peace; it's an actual blessing. It is the fullness of life as the Father intended, full of love, harmony, wholeness, and divine peace that guards our minds and hearts in Christ Jesus.

Philippians 4:7 speaks of the peace that "surpasses all understanding," a divine calm that guards our hearts and minds even during life's storms.

When grounded in this peace, our joy cannot easily be stolen by life's challenges. Consider Jesus, asleep in the boat during a raging storm (Matthew 8:23-27). *"As he got into the boat, his disciples followed him. Suddenly, a violent storm arose on the sea, so that the boat was being swamped by the waves—but Jesus kept sleeping. So the disciples came and woke him up, saying, "Lord, save us! We're going to die!" He said to them, "Why are you afraid, you of little faith?" Then he got up and rebuked the winds and the sea, and there was a great calm. The men were amazed and asked, What kind of man is this?*

Even the winds and the sea obey him!"

While His disciples panicked, Jesus, in his humanity, was calm and resting in the boat, asleep, in fact displaying how to move in faith, reminding us that the storms in our lives don't have to cause us to turn our worlds upside down. There's a peace that's rooted in trust— and from this place, trust flows unshakable joy. We, too, are called to rest in this peace, confident that God is in control at all times.

Patience: The Simmering of Joy

Patience can be a virtue many struggle with at first— I've become much more patient over the years, but still have work to do…it's truly a process! However, the benefits that are gained from this virtue are priceless. It's the quiet strength that helps us endure life's delays, frustrations, and challenges without losing our cool. Patience is often tested unexpectedly, like when you're running late and the slowest driver on the planet pulls in front of you.

But patience does more than keep us from honking the horn or snapping at our kids. It allows joy to simmer and grow over time. Patience and peace go hand in hand; when we're patient, we accept that we're not in control—and that's okay. Trusting in God's perfect timing brings joy even in seasons of waiting.

As James 1:2-3 reminds us:

"Consider it pure joy, my brothers and sisters, whenever you face trials of many kinds, because you know that the testing of your faith produces perseverance." One of the ways the Lord has taught me patience is through waiting for him to answer my prayers. In this fast-paced, microwave society, I have been tempted to expect God to answer me immediately when I pray. How about you? And at times that's exactly what happened. Other times, it's as if He didn't hear my request at all. In those times, I found that the answers would come when I'd let the desires I wanted fall away and surrender to what He wanted for my life. It was in trusting that He knows best what I needed at that time. I've come to understand that I can thank Him for the no's, on those things I really desired, but He knew it would not have been good for me, and He planned to give me something better if I was willing to wait on Him. The things I've received by waiting and being patient are actually mind-blowing. As I look back over my life, they make me shout for joy! Because I couldn't see the whole picture. He is so faithful, and it's worth every effort to learn how to wait and patiently trust what He has for us. His ways and thoughts are so much higher than ours. It's so worthwhile, and joy will bubble up in the anticipation of His goodness as we learn to be patient.

Gentleness: The Quiet Power of Joy

Gentleness is an often overlooked attribute of the Spirit, but it is vital in cultivating joy. It's not weakness; it's strength under control. Jesus demonstrated gentleness in all He did, leaving people not only healed but also filled with joy.

Consider the story of the woman caught in adultery (John 8:1-11). Picture this scene: A group of men throws her at Jesus' feet, ready to stone her for her sins.

They demand that Jesus join them in their condemnation, but instead, He responds with extraordinary gentleness. He bends down, writes something mysterious in the dirt, and then says, *"Let any one of you who is without sin be the first to throw a stone at her."* One by one, her accusers walk away, and Jesus, in His

gentle mercy, says to her, *"Neither do I condemn you. Go now and leave your life of sin."*

Imagine the joy she must have felt—joy born of mercy, forgiveness, and gentleness. When we act gently toward others, we reflect Christ's love. It's a powerful reminder that, as believers, we are called to embody Christ's gentleness in a world that is often harsh and unforgiving.

In Scripture, gentleness is translated prautēs (also meaning "meekness"), which means strength under control, as mentioned earlier, but it's not weakness or passivity. It's the humble, patient, and controlled way to handle ourselves, especially when provoked. True wisdom is often displayed through a gentle spirit. For example, giving a gentle answer in the heat of an argument can diffuse anger at the root. It allows the flames of anger fire, to dissipate, instead of becoming an inferno that rages out of control. Meekness allows us to be the calm in the midst of an emotional storm.

It allows us to bear one another's flaws with grace and love. Our true strength and maturity in Christ is a witness to others when we can control our tongues, even when we have every right to lash back, but we choose not to. It's the Spirit-powered restraint that chooses humility over pride, patience over irritation, and mercy over judgment; it's our ability to reflect Jesus to those around us.

Joy and Self-Control: A Surprising Pair

At first, self-control might not seem connected to joy, but it plays a crucial role. Proverbs 25:28 warns us, *"Like a city whose walls are broken through is a person who lacks self-control."* Without self-control, joy can be stolen by impulsive decisions or unchecked emotions. Exercising self-control keeps our focus on God's promises rather than temporary frustrations. It allows us to pause before reacting and protects the joy God has placed within us. Think about it: how many times have you felt regret after losing your temper or indulging in something that later left you feeling empty? Exercising self-control helps us live in a way that aligns with God's will—and that alignment naturally brings joy. Self-control in scripture is from the Greek word "enkrateia," meaning mastery over one's desires and impulses. It's not just our willpower; however, it's the empowerment of the Holy Spirit that governs our thoughts, actions, and emotions so they align with God's perfect will for our lives. It's the ability to say "Yes" to the Father's will, when our emotions are screaming, "No!" Self-control shows up on those days, we decide to be quiet when we want to make our point in a discussion or dispute. James 1:19 urges us to be *"quick to listen, slow to speak, and slow to anger."* It's the power to control our appetites and desires. It's when we say, "No, I won't have that third piece of cake," because diabetes runs in my family. Yes, I can apologize, even though I feel I did nothing wrong. Self-control helps us set boundaries against sins tactics, that try to take us off God's course and steal our joy. It frees us from being ruled by our emotions once we master it. It will help build a reputation of trust and credibility that others come to rely on. Self-control helps us to walk in victory as we follow Christ. Which leads us back to joy in the surrender.

How Joy Releases Who We Truly Are

Now, you might be wondering: how does joy release more of who we truly are? Great question! Joy rooted in the Holy Spirit aligns us with God's nature. Since we are made in His image (Genesis 1:27), the more joy we cultivate, the more we reflect His character. Joy energizes us to serve others, endure trials, and rest in God's promises. It frees us from fear, anxiety, and bitterness, allowing us to live authentically as God designed us. When we live in joy, we become a light to the world, showing others the beauty of life in Christ.

It's about embracing our authentic and true identity that can only be found in the one who created us. The Father designed each of us so uniquely, and it's in this creative difference that we find joy in ourselves, and it brings joy into others' lives as they interact with us. Being unique is a gift that we must learn to understand and use to our advantage. There is only one you the world will ever see, and it's important not to hide our uniqueness from the world. It's our time to shine bright in the earth to display the goodness and glory of our Father. You are a special reflection of Him that no other person can display. You are God's masterpiece, created to do good works that he planned for you to do before He ever sent you to the earth. (Eph 2:10) There are "miracles" you hold within you. Your unique and individual talents and gifts need to come through you from heaven into the earth. No one else can do that "thing" you do; you are the only one, and the world is waiting on you to do it. It's a hidden treasure buried deep within you that God wants to bring out. So it's time to start searching for that gold you have within, it's called the kingdom of God that's within you. There are treasures in this earth in vessels that the master artist is trying to show off. So we can't be intimidated by what the world says is valuable and not do what the Lord is asking us to do because it doesn't fit into societal norms. What you have is actually designed to confound the wisdom of this world. When you find and start doing that thing God created you to do, it will shock you and the world. Everyone will be sitting there shaking their heads because it will really be the anointing (Holy Spirit) showing out through you, as you partner with Him. This is how we bring and give all the Glory to our King! This is how those in darkness come to know about the good news of what God has done for us. This is how we live a life full of great joy. You were created to shine so bright that heaven is experienced on earth through you. We, as children of God, are His glory carriers, and he desires to partner with us to spread more love, more hope, more peace, and more joy! Knowing you are one of a kind should make us sing and shout with joy.

Let joy be the song that rises in your heart, for as Psalm 118:24 declares: *"This is the day the Lord has made; let us rejoice and be glad in it."*

JOY NUGGET

The more we **SURRENDER** to God's will for our lives, the more beautiful and sweet the essence of joy will flow in and through us. It's not through our efforts and strength, but it's the work of the Holy Spirit. **We don't have to force joy—it manifests as we ABIDE in His love** by staying close to His heart.

DRAWING CLOSER

Joy is not a formula; it's the fruit of the spirit being developed in the believer's life each day by abiding in our creator. We do this through prayer, studying in the scriptures, worshipping, and daily dependence by following His plans for our lives. It requires trust and the ability to rest in Him for all we need. When we do this, we will notice significant changes in our lives as we become more like Jesus.

"How can I trust Jesus to release more of His spirit in my life, to lead and guide me this week?"

Scripture Reading (John 15)

Let's Pray:

Heavenly Father,

Thank You for being a God of love and for making joy a part of Your divine nature. Thank You for planting the seeds of joy within us when we became Your children.

We are grateful that You water these seeds, growing them into mighty fruit trees that bless not only our lives but also the lives of everyone we encounter. May we spread the seeds of love and joy wherever we go, transforming this world for Your glory.

Help us live in peace, walk in patience, show gentleness, and exercise self-control, as we come to understand our uniqueness and this hidden treasure within, allowing us to bring it out and glorify your holy name. Allow joy to flow through us. Thank You for Your unending grace and for giving us the strength to reflect Your light. In Jesus' name, Amen.

> *Those who **SOW** in tears will reap with **SHOUTS** of joy.*
>
> Psalm 126:5 (CSB)

Reflection & Revelation to Remember

CHAPTER 8

Joy in Giving

Generosity That Produces Joy

Generosity is a profound theme woven throughout the Bible, like a golden thread in the intricate tapestry of God's love and grace. God Himself is the epitome of generosity—a Father who loves His children so deeply that He gave His only Son, Jesus Christ, as a sacrifice for the world (John 3:16). Now, that is mindblowing generosity! Could anything be more radical? This is the heart of the gospel—God gave, and His giving produces joy, salvation, and life for all who believe.

In our lives, we are called to reflect this divine generosity. Have you ever met someone who is a radical giver? Not the person who gives a few dollars here and there, but someone who gives until it costs them something significant. Such givers inspire us, making us pause and reflect, "Am I doing enough? Can I be more like them?"

As we will explore, radical generosity doesn't just bless others—it transforms us from the inside out, producing joy that mirrors the joy of Christ Himself.

The Radical Example of King David

One of the clearest examples of radical giving in the Bible is found in 1 Chronicles 29, where King David prepares for the construction of God's Temple. David didn't just contribute a small portion of his wealth—he gave extravagantly, both from the nation's treasury and his personal fortune. His offerings included 100 tons of gold and 250 tons of silver. To put that in today's terms, that's about $256 billion in gold alone! Talk about jaw-dropping! Imagine how CNN would cover that story today: "President Donates Billions for Heavenly Kingdom Building Project—Economists Baffled." Yet, David's heart was not in building his own kingdom on earth, but in honoring God by bringing heaven's agenda to earth; this should be our aim as well.

What's even more amazing is the domino effect David's generosity had. His radical giving stirred the hearts of the people. Leaders, soldiers, and ordinary citizens followed his lead, contributing more gold, silver, bronze, and iron—enough to build the Temple and then some! Collectively, they gave 185 tons of gold and 375 tons of silver. And what happened next? Joy broke out among the people! It wasn't just fleeting happiness—it was a deep, abiding joy that came from a place of sacrificial giving.

This story shows that radical generosity is contagious. It spreads like wildfire, inspiring others to give as well. As the people gave, they were filled with joy, and David rejoiced greatly. I can almost hear David now, saying to the Lord, "Look at Your people! Look how they've given from their hearts!" And surely, the Father was smiling down, well-pleased, saying, "This is a reflection of My own heart."

Joy and Generosity: A Heavenly Connection

Why does generosity produce joy? Because giving connects us to the heart of God. Our Father is the ultimate giver. He gives us life, breath, and every good thing. Most importantly, He gave us Jesus, the greatest gift of all. When we give, we tap into this divine nature. In a sense, we are imitating our Heavenly Father by modeling this giving nature as well. He's our example of how to be the perfect giver, showing us how when He dwelt amongst us on the earth.

In Philippians 2:6-8, we read about Jesus, who, though He was God, didn't cling to His divine status. Instead, He gave up everything, becoming a servant and humbling Himself even to the point of death on a cross. Jesus' life was marked by radical generosity—He gave His life for us. And He did it with joy! Hebrews 12:2

says, *"For the joy set before Him, He endured the cross."* Jesus' joy wasn't in the suffering itself, but in what His suffering would accomplish—our salvation and reconciliation to the Father. When we give generously, we become more like Jesus, highlighting a joy that transcends circumstances.

However, in reality, left to our own devices, we are often selfish. Our natural inclination is to hold on tightly to what we have, whether it's our money, our time, or our resources.

Generosity doesn't come naturally—it requires intentionality. For some of us, God has given a special grace to be exceptionally generous, but for most of us, it's something we need to grow into. It requires trust—trust that God will provide for us when we give. The more we trust Him, the easier our giving will become.

God's Blessing Through Giving

Generosity doesn't just bless the recipient—it blesses the giver. In Luke 6:38, Jesus tells us, *"Give, and it will be given to you. A good measure, pressed down, shaken together, and running over, will be poured into your lap. For with the measure you use, it will be measured back to you."* In other words, you can't out-give God. The more you give, the more He blesses you, often in ways you wouldn't expect.

I've witnessed this in my own life and in the lives of others. Time and time again, when people give out of faith, trusting God to meet their needs, He shows up in remarkable ways. Giving is like planting seeds in a garden; you will see a harvest from what you've sown eventually. It might be a financial blessing, or it might be an emotional or spiritual one. Sometimes, the blessing is simply the joy and contentment that come from knowing you've made a difference in someone's life. The Bible tells us, (Matt 6:3-4) *"But when you give to the poor, don't let your left hand know what your right hand is doing, so that your giving may be in secret. And your Father who sees in secret will reward you."* When we bless others with our giving, we should aim to do it secretly whenever possible and not to impress others. When we do, the Father will reward us openly in the way He sees fit, which is so much more beneficial than the reward of trying to make ourselves seem important by our outward show of giving.

There's also something deeply liberating about being generous. It frees us from the clutches of materialism. You know that constant itch to have more? The endless cycle of wanting the latest gadget, the newest car, the bigger house? If we're not careful, that's a fast track to misery, my friend. The Apostle Paul hits the nail on the head in 1 Timothy 6:6 when he says, *"Godliness with contentment is great gain."* Generosity helps us break free from the chains of "keeping up with the Joneses" and instead find joy in what truly matters. Things like our physical and mental health, family and friends we spend time with on a regular basis, having our daily needs met, and not just living in survival mode. I've found that no one ever looks back on their life when they are about to depart earth and says, "I wish I had bought that Ferrari, or a bigger house." But they might say, "I wish my children were here with me now, I wish I could have more time, to show those I love, how much I really do love them in practical ways." Remembering how blessed we already are helps keep us balanced. Eventually, we will realize "more stuff" is not the answer to contentment; being in His presence is.

Treasures in Heaven

Jesus speaks about storing up treasures in heaven in Matthew 6:20: *"Store up for yourselves treasures in heaven, where moths and vermin do not destroy, and where thieves do not break in and steal."* Earthly treasures are temporary, but heavenly treasures are eternal. When we give generously, we are making investments in eternity. Every act of kindness, every gift given in love, is like depositing into our heavenly bank account. The Father is

keeping a record of our generosity and the love we pour out onto others. As His children, we reflect His goodness, and being generous is one of the easiest ways to show the love of God to others on the earth.

Now, I don't know about you, but I'd rather have a hefty balance in my heavenly account than in my earthly one. After all, this life is just a vapor compared to eternity. The things we do here—especially our acts of generosity—have a far greater impact than we realize.

Imagine arriving in heaven and hearing God say, "Well done, good and faithful servant." I'd trade all the riches of this world to hear those words. And if being generous is part of what it takes to get there, count me in!

Faith and Generosity Go Hand in Hand

Being a radical giver requires faith. Let's face it—giving when you have plenty is one thing, but giving when you're in need yourself, that's a whole other level. It requires trusting God to meet your needs when you're helping to meet someone else's. In Philippians 4:19, Paul assures us, *"And my God will meet all your needs according to the riches of His glory in Christ Jesus."* God knows what we need, and He promises to provide. ("God's Promises - KJIC")

But remember, we need to believe Him. Giving is an act of faith. It's saying, "God, I trust You to take care of me as I take care of others." Faith is like a muscle, and it must be exercised in order to grow. When it comes to giving, it requires stepping out, being a blessing to others, as the Lord leads, then trusting

Him for the results. And the more we trust Him, the more we see His faithfulness. Over time, this builds our faith and deepens our joy. It becomes easier to give because we've experienced firsthand how God takes care of His children. There was a time when I was really struggling, it was back in 2008 when the housing crash happened, and things were a struggle for a lot of people. Someone found out about my circumstances and donated groceries to me, and I was so elated. Then I heard the Lord say, I want you to give half of those groceries to your neighbor. "What? ... but they're fine," I thought to myself, and can I tell you my flesh didn't want to obey. But I did what I believed I heard the Lord say, and joy came over me as I walked to bless my neighbor. It turned out they did need the help after all, and because I obeyed the Holy Spirit, we both got blessed by that donation. Not only that, but the remaining food seemed to stretch. It seemed like I had those groceries for weeks, as if they multiplied. That's what happens when faith and giving mix together...we can expect miracles!

The Joy of God's Faithfulness

If you've never seen God's faithfulness in the area of giving, I encourage you to give it a try. In Malachi 3:10, God actually invites us to test Him in our giving. He says, *"Bring the whole tithe into the storehouse... Test me in this and see if I will not throw open the floodgates of heaven and pour out so much blessing that there will not be room enough to store it.*" This is a law He set up on the earth, that works for anyone who will act upon it. It's the law of sowing and reaping, which tells us that whatever we do will eventually come back to us, whether it be good or bad. Now, that's something to really ponder, because when the Creator of the universe invites us to test Him in our giving, I'm intrigued! And can I tell you, I've seen His hand of provision come through for me every time in the end. When we give generously, we will also reap generously, and the opposite is also true.

Start small if you need to. Maybe it's a small donation to someone in need or an extra gift to your favorite organization. Perhaps it's your time or talents that you give freely. As you step out in faith, you'll begin to see God's hand at work in your life. And as you witness His faithfulness, your joy will overflow. You'll discover the truth of Jesus' words: *"It is more blessed to give than to receive"* (Acts 20:35). And the best part? You'll find that no matter how much you give, God always gives back more.

A Life of Joyful Giving

Highlights to remember: generosity aligns us with God's purposes, blesses others, and releases joy into our lives. It frees us from materialism, deepens our trust in God, and allows us to store up treasures in heaven.

And most importantly, it makes us more like Jesus, the ultimate giver.

So, let's strive to be radical givers. Let's give in ways that stretch us—ways that make us rely on God to meet our needs. Let's be people who reflect the generous heart of our Father in heaven. And as we do, we'll discover a joy that is unshakable, a joy that comes not from what we have, but from what we give.

In the words of C.S. Lewis, "Nothing you have not given away will ever be really yours." So, give joyfully, give generously, and watch how God blesses you beyond measure. You may just find that the more you give, the more joy you receive.

JOY NUGGET

JOY flows freely when we give it away; it becomes a river of joy for others, not just a reservoir of God's goodness that blesses us alone or our resources. Generosity isn't just about giving monetarily either; it's about living open-handed with our time, talents, and our presence in service to others, along with our resources. **Giving mixed with our faith is a conduit to the miracle-working power of God,** allowing it to flow in our lives as well as bless others. The Father wants to partner with us; in fact, the Holy Spirit is eager to help us, so we can display His glory. Through radical giving as kingdom ambassadors, we become His change agents, who shift our communities and regions, helping to advance His kingdom agenda in the earth. May we endeavor to give generously like King David, and better yet, **become an extravagant giver like our Father in heaven!**

DRAWING CLOSER

Take some time to reflect on the extravagant gift that was given to you by Jesus. He decided to lay down His life for our sins. Reflect on the things you've done. All the things no one knows about, and you think you got away with. Can I tell you,

Jesus knows and saw it all. And yet, because of His love, when we repent, He is faithful to forgive us and reconcile us back to the Father. Jesus gave us the ultimate gift of His sacrifice. Our amazing creator is our perfect example of how to be a radical giver. We were created to reflect His nature as givers, here on earth. To focus on our kingdom assignments over our own agendas. This week, find a few creative ways to give back. For example, you could encourage a depressed friend or take them out to dinner. Offer a ride to someone. Watch a single mom's child for a few hours, etc. The possibilities are endless. Then examine how much joy arises in your heart as a result. This is how we release the heart of the Father and spread joy to others by being radical givers, like our King.

Scripture Reading (Luke 6)

Let's Pray:

Heavenly Father,

We thank You for making us in Your image, because You are the ultimate giver. You gave us Your Son to die for us, and we are grateful. Help us to always remember the sacrifice You've made for us as we look to You in our giving. We know that giving doesn't come naturally, so we ask You to change our hearts and create in us a pure heart that's more like Yours, a heart that wants to give and release all that You are asking of us. May we bring glory to Your holy name as we stretch and grow in our ability to give, and may we one day hear You say,

"Well done, good and faithful servant!" Amen.

> *When I am filled with cares, your **COMFORT** brings me joy.*
>
> Psalm 94:19 (CSB)

Reflection & Revelation to Remember

CHAPTER 9

Joy and Resilience

How Adversity Builds Strength

At first glance, we may not immediately see joy and resilience as interconnected concepts. However, when we take a closer look, we realize that they are more intertwined than we initially thought. Resilience is often defined as "the ability to withstand or recover quickly from difficulties; toughness." This toughness is essential for followers of Jesus, especially in today's world. Since the pandemic, it feels as though we barely catch our breath before we're faced with the next crisis. In this fast-paced environment, the ability to bounce back and adapt quickly to adverse challenges is no longer just a valuable skill—it's a necessity.

When we examine the life of Nehemiah, we see a man deeply moved by the plight of the survivors who had been exiled from Jerusalem, a city now in ruins with its walls broken down and gates burned. Upon hearing this distressing news, Nehemiah was overcome with sorrow, weeping and mourning for days. He turned to prayer and fasting, seeking guidance from the Lord. At that time, Nehemiah served as an official cupbearer to King Artaxerxes of Persia.

The King noticed Nehemiah's sadness and inquired about the cause, suspecting it was a sickness of the heart since

Nehemiah was not physically ill. Nehemiah explained the plight of his people and the city he loved. Upon hearing this, the King granted him favor to rebuild the city. Nehemiah then devised a plan and began the reconstruction. However, he faced resistance from several adversaries who mocked, threatened, and plotted against him. Despite this, Nehemiah prayed continually and trusted in God. He instructed his builders to carry tools in one hand and weapons in the other, as they had to fight and work simultaneously to rebuild the wall. Despite the discouragement and schemes of others, Nehemiah stood strong in resilience and achieved victory. A beautiful truth we can hold onto from this story is, *"The joy of the Lord is your strength"* (Nehemiah 8:10).

Isn't that an uplifting reminder? Our strength doesn't come from gritting our teeth and pushing through on our own. Instead, it comes from the joy we find in the Lord—a joy that helps us withstand the challenges we face. This joy doesn't fluctuate with our circumstances;

it is a steadfast, eternal joy rooted in our trust and relationship with the Father.

God Carries Our Burdens

Now, I'm sure you've heard this before, but let me ask you: Do you really know that you don't have to carry your burdens alone? It's so easy to nod and agree with that concept in theory, but do you live it out? I used to think I had to solve every problem myself. Let me tell you, trying to be a superhero isn't as fun as it looks! It's exhausting, truthfully… we don't have enough time for that. Eventually, I learned that trying to manage everything on my own only leads to one thing—more stress.

That's why 1 Peter 5:7 hit me like a ton of bricks: *"Cast all your anxiety on Him because He cares for you."* Wait a minute, you mean I don't have to do this on my own? God says, "Cast all your anxiety on Him." What? …I can literally lay all these problems down at Jesus' feet and let Him handle them? Where do I sign up for that? If you're like me—a fixer, a doer—this scripture can be life-changing. It's a relief to know that we have divine help to manage the demands of life. The Bible says we have a helper, the Holy Spirit, who is always available to assist us. When we release our heavy burdens and trust God, not only do we find rest, but those around us—our family and friends—benefit from our more peaceful and joyful spirit, as well.

The Connection Between Joy and Resilience

The joy of the Lord fuels resilience. When we let go of the need to control everything and embrace God's strength, we are better equipped to face life's challenges. Adversity often feels like a storm, but through faith, we find that joy anchors us. It doesn't mean the storms stop; it means we know they won't overtake us.

Each time we rely on God, our resilience grows. Like a muscle that strengthens through repeated use, our spiritual toughness increases every time we trust Him to carry us through adversity. As a result, our lives begin to reflect His peace and power, inspiring others to seek the same strength.

So, let's stop striving to be superheroes and instead lean on the ultimate strength giver—Jesus. Through joy, we can build the resilience we need to navigate life's difficulties with grace, strength, and peace.

Trials Tend to Come in Clusters

Have you ever noticed that challenges don't come one at a time? It's like the enemy waits for the perfect moment to release a flood of chaos into our lives. The car breaks down, student loans are due, and a work crisis hits—all in the same week! It can feel overwhelming. Yet, even in these moments, we have to remember that God is sovereign, and He sees everything we're going through.

Here's a comforting thought: the enemy can't mess with you without God's permission. Yes, that's right, the devil must ask permission before he can bring any harm against us in any way. As Job 1:12 says, *"The Lord said to Satan, 'All right, do whatever you want with anything that he has, but don't hurt Job himself."* We can see here that there was a limit to what God allowed to happen to Job, and it's the same for us. And here's the best part: we're already wired to overcome whatever the enemy throws at us. In fact, we're more than equipped to handle adversity because of who we are in Christ.

When we face trials, it's easy to lose sight of our true identity as children of God. But remembering who we are in Jesus helps us keep our joy intact, even during hard times. James 1:2-3 tells us to *"consider it pure joy...whenever you face trials of many kinds, because you know that the testing of your faith produces perseverance."* Trials, believe it or not, are designed to strengthen us. When we come into God's family, we have access to our true identity. It started the day we put our trust and hope in Jesus. On that day, you became a child of God and literally signed up to become a warrior. Surprise! I know a lot of churches don't discuss these things up front or tell you the full story about this invisible war, and many have been caught off guard. But the truth is, you were made for war! Your actual DNA now carries the

Complete Joy

imprint of the Father; you are a light barrier designed to eradicate the darkness. Your mission is to fight the good fight of faith against a cosmic battle of spiritual beings that hate you. You do this by renewing your mind and learning the truth of God's word through the bible. The bible is no ordinary book, like this one you're reading. The bible is alive and active and sharper than any two-edged sword, dividing the intentions of our hearts. It will illuminate and reveal things you need when you need them. It will expose darkness in you and others, and it will light the path to Truth, which is Jesus himself. He is our guide. He knows how to win this war; in fact, it's already won. Hallelujah! The word is your compass for navigating this life while on earth. And your enemy will do everything in his power to stop you from reading it and taking it in truth. You must fight this resistance and know that the Holy Spirit is ready to assist you in winning. So, why am I bringing this all up? Because one of the tactics of the enemy is to bring trial

after trial to get you so bogged down with the things of this world that you lose focus on the real fight going on above your head. We can easily look at our current circumstances and forget that most of our trials don't matter as much as they seem. We have been given authority to control what happens to us through prayer and petition in the heavenly realms. We can cause things to shift or be halted completely when we know and walk in our full authority. So, a lot of times, the enemy will distract you to the point you never find out how powerful a warrior you really are, because he knows when you come into that understanding, it's game over for him. This is why knowing that trials build our character, our endurance, and yes, even our joy is so important. Through adversity, we become more like Jesus, who endured the ultimate hardship for the joy set before Him (Hebrews 12:2). We will never have to endure as much as Jesus; however, it's encouraging to know that we are able to endure much more than we realize, as we trust the Father, knowing He is helping us stay strong through every trial. And joy awaits us at the finish line.

Adversity Makes Us More Like Jesus

Speaking of Jesus, can we take a moment to reflect on His life? He faced more adversity than any of us will ever know. From being misunderstood by His own family, betrayed by a close friend, and ultimately dying a gruesome death on the cross, Jesus' life was filled with suffering. But why did He endure it? Hebrews 12:2 tells us, *"For the joy set before Him, He endured the cross, scorning its shame, and sat down at the right hand of the throne of God."*

Jesus knew that the suffering He endured on the cross was not in vain. It wasn't the end of the story. He looked ahead to the joy that would come from being reunited with His Father—and with us. Isn't that mindblowing? Jesus endured unimaginable pain for the joy of bringing us back into a relationship with God.

If Jesus can endure the cross for the joy set before Him, then we, too, can endure our own trials with the hope of future joy. And let's not forget that we have the Holy Spirit living inside of us, helping us every step of the way. The challenges we face in this life pale in comparison to the eternal reward awaiting us in heaven. As 2 Corinthians 4:17 reminds us, *"For our light and momentary troubles are achieving for us an eternal glory that far outweighs them all."*

The Refining Fire of Adversity

God doesn't allow adversity in our lives to break us. On the contrary, He allows it to shape and refine us. 1 Peter 1:6-7 compares our faith to gold that is refined by fire: *"These have come so that the proven genuineness of your faith—of greater worth than gold, which perishes even though refined by fire—may result in praise, glory, and honor when Jesus Christ is revealed."*

Have you ever watched a blacksmith at work? They heat the metal until it's glowing red, then hammer it into shape. It's a tough process, but the result is a tool that is strong, durable, and useful. That's what adversity does for us. It purifies our faith, strips away the things that don't matter, and leaves us stronger and more focused on God's purposes. Malachi 3:3 says, *"He will be like a refiner and purifier of silver; he will purify the sons of Levi and refine them like gold and silver."*

In the heat of adversity, it's easy to forget that we're being refined. It's uncomfortable, sometimes painful, but it's not without purpose. God is working in us, molding us into vessels that can carry His glory and fulfill His purposes. And just like gold that comes out of the fire shining and valuable, we emerge from adversity stronger, wiser, with the resemblance of Jesus on our countenance. So, learn to embrace the fiery trials and use them to your advantage. By becoming all that the Father has created you to be. With every victory, joy awaits you on the other side.

Humility Through Adversity

Adversity has a way of humbling us, doesn't it? When we face challenges we can't solve on our own, we're reminded that we are not as self-sufficient as we'd like to think. And that's a good thing! Humility is one of the most important virtues we can develop as followers of Christ. In fact, the Bible says in Job 5:17, *"Blessed is the one whom God corrects; so do not despise the discipline of the Almighty."* God's correction is a gift we must learn to respect and even desire. It's from His love for us that he corrects and leads us on the right path. Like any loving parent who protects their child, our heavenly Father will redirect us when we go off the path he has designed for us. Knowing this causes us to trust the process, knowing that as we lean on Him, we will fulfill the purpose He's created for us to flourish in.

When we humble ourselves and ask for help, God is quick to come to our aid. He doesn't leave us to flounder in our struggles. Instead, He uses our mistakes and failures to teach us and make us wiser. And truthfully, sometimes we need those humbling moments to remind us that we don't have it all figured out. Humility opens the door to growth, and growth leads to joy.

Adversity Clarifies Our Purpose

Another incredible benefit of adversity is that it has a way of clearing out the clutter in our lives and helping us focus on what really matters. When we're faced with a tough situation, it forces us to reevaluate our priorities. What is truly important? What distractions have been pulling us away from our purpose? Adversity strips away the nonessentials and helps us focus on our God-given mission.

In the midst of trials, we often find that our values become clearer, and we gain a renewed sense of purpose. This is part of the refining process that God allows us to go through. And when we come out on the other side, we're more focused, more intentional, and more aligned with God's will.

1 Peter 1:6-7 reminds us that our faith, like pure gold, is refined through trials. It's in these challenging seasons that our faith is proven genuine, and we emerge more focused on our divine calling. Our trials help us become the people God created us to be—refined, purified, and ready to fulfill His purposes on the earth.

God Works All Things for Good

One of the most comforting promises in Scripture is found in Romans 8:28: *"And we know that in all things God works for the good of those who love Him, who have been called according to His purpose."* God is always working behind the scenes, taking even the most difficult circumstances and using them for our good and His glory.

It's important to remember this when we're in the midst of adversity. When everything seems to be going wrong, it can be easy to lose hope. But God's Word reassures us that He is in control, and He is working things out for our good. No challenge is wasted. Every trial we face is an opportunity for growth, strengthening our faith, and becoming more like Jesus. He is refining us, strengthening us, and preparing us for greater things.

And as we lean on Him, we experience the joy that comes from knowing we are in His hands.

At the end of the day, adversity is not something to be feared. Yes, it's tough. Yes, it's uncomfortable. But it's process, knowing that as we lean on Him, we will fulfill the purpose He's created for us to flourish in.

When we humble ourselves and ask for help, God is quick to come to our aid. He doesn't leave us to flounder in our struggles. Instead, He uses our mistakes and failures to teach us and make us wiser. And truthfully, sometimes we need those humbling moments to remind us that we don't have it all figured out. Humility opens the door to growth, and growth leads to joy.

Adversity Clarifies Our Purpose

Another incredible benefit of adversity is that it has a way of clearing out the clutter in our lives and helping us focus on what really matters. When we're faced with a tough situation, it forces us to reevaluate our priorities. What is truly important? What distractions have been pulling us away from our purpose? Adversity strips away the nonessentials and helps us focus on our God-given mission.

In the midst of trials, we often find that our values become clearer, and we gain a renewed sense of purpose. This is part of the refining process that God allows us to go through. And when we come out on the other side, we're more focused, more intentional, and more aligned with God's will.

1 Peter 1:6-7 reminds us that our faith, like pure gold, is refined through trials. It's in these challenging seasons that our faith is proven genuine, and we emerge more focused on our divine calling. Our trials help us become the people God created us to be—refined, purified, and ready to fulfill His purposes on the earth.

God Works All Things for Good

One of the most comforting promises in Scripture is found in Romans 8:28: *"And we know that in all things God works for the good of those who love Him, who have been called according to His purpose."* God is always working behind the scenes, taking even the most difficult circumstances and using them for our good and His glory.

It's important to remember this when we're in the midst of adversity. When everything seems to be going wrong, it can be easy to lose hope. But God's Word reassures us that He is in control, and He is working things out for our good. No challenge is wasted. Every trial we face is an opportunity for growth, strengthening our faith, and becoming more like Jesus. He is refining us, strengthening us, and preparing us for greater things.

And as we lean on Him, we experience the joy that comes from knowing we are in His hands.

At the end of the day, adversity is not something to be feared. Yes, it's tough. Yes, it's uncomfortable. But it's also an incredible opportunity for growth. And in the midst of it all, we find joy—joy in knowing that God is with us, that He is refining us, and that He is working all things for our good.

So the next time life throws you a curveball, take heart. Remember that adversity builds strength, produces joy, and by keeping our eyes on Jesus, joy will become strength, and most importantly, know that no matter what comes your way, God has already equipped you to overcome. In Him, you are resilient, and through Him, you can endure.

JOY NUGGET

When your joy is rooted in Jesus, you will bend and not break. He becomes the anchor for your soul to rest upon, and His love will guide and direct every path you should take. It's when we learn to rest in him, we find our peace and strength to endure the most difficult situations. **Our resilience comes in knowing we can trust Him.**

DRAWING CLOSER

Spend some time reflecting on a time Jesus showed up for you during a trial. What did that look like? How did you feel loved by His support? How were you resilient and able to keep going even though it was tough? Remind yourself today that discipleship is about trusting Jesus and His way again and again. It's about getting back in the fight when you're tired and worn out, understanding you are made to win this war. You are growing stronger in your weakness and learning to embrace the help of the Holy Spirit to give you strength, which leads you back to joy.

Scripture Reading (Nehemiah 8)

Let's Pray:

Heavenly Father,

Thank You that You will never leave us nor forsake us, even in the midst of a trial when we feel as though we are alone. We know You are working on our behalf. We thank You in advance for equipping us to overcome every challenge we will face in the future, because You are fighting for us! We know that the same Spirit that raised Jesus from the grave lives in us now, so we are more than capable of doing everything You ask of us, even the hard things. We praise You for making us warriors who will fight the good fight and never give up. Amen.

> *Rejoice in the **LORD** always. I will say it again: **REJOICE!***
>
> Philippians 4:4 (CSB)

Reflection & Revelation to Remember

CHAPTER 10

The Key to Joy

Worship as the Key

Worship is so powerful that it could easily be the focus of an entire book! (And trust me, I've been tempted.) For now, let's explore why worship is essential and how incorporating it into your daily life can unlock a wellspring of joy and peace. After all, who couldn't use more of both? Let's examine the key of David that's found in Rev 3:7-8, it says, *"Write to the angel of the church in Philadelphia: Thus says the Holy One, the true one, the one who has the key of David, who opens and no one will close, and who closes and no one opens: I know your works. Look, I have placed before you an open door that no one can close because you have but little power; yet you have kept my word and have not denied my name.*" Jesus is the true and holy one, who holds the key to our access. Whatever He opens, no one can shut; whatever He shuts, no one can open. This means there are promises for our lives that were written down before we even got here that no one can stop us from walking in, except ourselves, through our free will. It's a personal open door, designed to help us reach our God given assignments for our mission, things He planned for us long ago. There are even doors for more spiritual authority and deeper access into his presence. We access these doors by faith and obedience to His word, not by striving, with all our own power or might. No, these doors open when we rest and trust in the Spirit of the Lord, through worship. This is worship that allows us to taste and see that the Lord is good! (Psalms 34:8) This is worship that aligns us with God's heart, and may we one day hear as David did, This is a man or woman after my own heart, Amen.

The Transformative Nature of Worship

True worship is not just a ritual—it's a transformative experience that connects us deeply with our Creator. It is the act of recognizing Jesus for His present work in our lives, His past faithfulness, and the promises He holds for the future. This recognition fills us with gratitude, which blossoms into joy—a joy rooted in God's sovereign nature, His love, and His power as the Creator of all things.

When we worship with sincerity, we acknowledge our absolute dependence on God. It's in this vulnerable space—where we lay down our pride and distractions— that joy begins to heal our hearts and transform our lives. Worship is not just about singing or outward expression; it's a posture of the heart that reorients us to God's presence and power. When we worship in spirit and in truth, we enter a realm of His glory where miracles will begin to transform our situations and circumstances. True worship will heal sickness in our bodies, destroy depression or anxiety, break off the spirit of fear and doubt, and strengthen our resolve to keep pushing forward in our assignments. True worship empowers us to shift our atmosphere. It's what allows heaven to invade the earth and change things around us for the better.

Worship Shifts Our Focus

Life's problems can feel like a heavy backpack— weighing us down, it's bulky, overpacked, and impossible to carry. Worship invites us to set our backpacks down at Jesus's feet. It redirects our focus from the weight of our struggles to the vastness of God's strength and goodness.

As Psalm 34:3 reminds us: *"Glorify the Lord with me; let us exalt His name together."* Worship lifts our eyes off our anxieties and helps us see the bigger picture— God's unfailing love, goodness, and peace. Suddenly, the challenges that seemed so overwhelming don't look quite as big anymore. By turning our focus from the problems of our struggles to the expansiveness of God's power, we experience a profound shift in perspective. It's like looking at those mountains of stress through the wrong end of a pair of binoculars—

what once seemed insurmountable now feels small and manageable in light of God's eternal plan.

Worship also reminds us that life's hardships are temporary. It lifts us into God's presence, where joy replaces worry, peace calms anxiety, and hope reigns supreme. As Matthew 6:33 teaches us, when we *"seek first the kingdom of God and His righteousness,"* everything else begins to fall into place. Worship aligns us with this truth, creating a ripple effect of peace and clarity in our daily lives. It's been proven that what we think

about and focus on the most is who we become. The life we experience starts in our minds with our thinking. The enemy loves to whisper lies to us, hoping we will believe them. But the Father has already given us our identity. We are designed to resemble Jesus. As we worship, we will begin to take on more of his character and nature. If we want to have a life full of joy and peace, we begin by aligning with God's will for our lives. Whatever He says about us is the truth, and we begin to recognize and realize this truth about ourselves the more we spend time in prayer and worship, by dwelling in His presence. Speaking of dwelling, true worship is not about checking off religious boxes every day with our daily devotional reading or our once-a-week attendance at the Sunday church service. (Matt 12:7-8) say's *"If you would not have condemned the innocent. For the Son of Man is Lord of the Sabbath."* Jesus was confronting the religious leaders of His day with the truth that true worship is not found in our empty rituals, God's heart is not satisfied with all our singing loudly, clapping our hands, and pretense. He desires mercy and compassion that flows from our heart like His, the kind of love that flows when we have a true encounter with Him. We show who He is when we extend compassion to one another, overlooking each other's flaws and loving each other just the way we are, but calling each other up higher to reflect His son. When we aim to heal and restore instead of judge and condemn, mercy can lift each other's burdens. We worship in mercy every time we show someone kindness, forgiveness, listen, and assist their needs, every act leading to love. Worship without mercy becomes noise; worship fueled by mercy becomes joy. When we choose mercy over judgment, His presence is made visible through love. Let mercy be the melody of your worship. How can you show compassion to someone today? Ask yourself, "Am I trying to perform for God's approval or focused on outward perfectionism?" "Do I have God's heart of mercy working in and through me?"

Practical Steps to Incorporate Worship

Start Your Day in Worship: Begin each morning with a song, a prayer, or a quiet moment of thanksgiving. This sets the tone for your day and centers your heart on God.

Create a Worship Playlist: Fill your environment with worship music that uplifts your spirit and reminds you of God's promises.

Worship Through Gratitude: Take time to reflect on God's goodness. Write down blessings through journaling, both big and small, to cultivate a heart of thankfulness.

Pause and Praise: In moments of stress, pause to offer a quick word of praise. This simple act can shift your focus back to God and His ability to handle your burdens.

Worship Frees Us

Worship is not just about acknowledging our need for God—it's also a powerful act of release and freedom.

In worship, the weight of life's burdens lifts, and we experience the kind of rest that only God can provide. It's like taking a deep breath and exhaling all the stress, anxiety, and worry we've been carrying.

Have you ever entered a worship service feeling crushed under the weight of your struggles, only to leave feeling lighter, freer, and renewed? That's the transformative power of worship. Jesus promises this relief in Matthew 11:28: *"Come to me, all you who are weary and burdened, and I will give you rest."* Worship is the pathway to that rest.

In worship, we let go of the pressure to have all the answers because we serve a God who does. What a relief that is! Worship invites us to exchange our stress for God's peace, our worry for His joy. Like David dancing before the Lord in 2 Samuel 6:14, we are called to worship with total abandonment and surrender. As a minister of dance, I've experienced the true freedom that comes from the full expression and movement of our bodies. You don't need to be a dancer either to experiment with this type of freedom. Dance is a way of engaging our whole being in our adoration of the Father. He delights to see our joy in communing with Him. I want to encourage you to give it a try sometime when you know no one's watching; it might just become a regular occurrence.

When we surrender everything at God's feet, we experience freedom. Chains of fear, anxiety, and doubt fall away, replaced by the joy and strength (Nehemiah 8:10). Through worship, we engage in a spiritual exchange: our brokenness for His wholeness, our weakness for His strength, our sorrow for His joy. The more we worship, the more we are set free.

The Joy of Surrender: Realizing Our Dependence on Him

True worship begins with the realization that we are utterly dependent on God. We can do absolutely nothing without Him; our next breath depends on His faithfulness and goodness. That's a sobering thought, and yet despite our flaws, the Creator of the universe desires a deep and intimate relationship with us. Isn't that overwhelming in the best way? He loves us not because we are perfect, but because He is good and we are His.

God's love is pure, unconditional, and deeply personal. He actively seeks us out, longing for us to draw near. As the Bible reminds us, His pursuit of us is relentless. Every encounter with His love transforms us, replacing fear and striving with the security of being fully known and fully loved.

If you've never felt this closeness with God, know that it's His deepest desire for you to experience it. His love doesn't come with strings or conditions; it only asks for your presence. There is nothing else on earth like it. Imagine the joy of being loved completely, just as you are, without any need to prove your worth. That's the kind of love found in true worship. This type of love is worth pursuing; it's worth giving up everything to find it, like we read about in (Matt 13:44), which says *"The kingdom of heaven is like a treasure, buried in a field, that a man found and reburied. Then, in his joy, he goes and sells everything he has and buys that field.*" Worship is our way of finding that hidden treasure that can only be found by seeking and coming to know the Father in all his goodness.

Worship as a Source of Strength

In worship, we recognize that our strength, wisdom, and hope come from God. As Jesus says in John 15:5: *"I am the vine; you are the branches. If you remain in me and I in you, you will bear much fruit; apart from me, you can do nothing."*

This dependence on God is not a weakness; it's our greatest source of strength and joy. Just as a branch cannot thrive without the vine, we cannot thrive without the life-giving connection to our Creator. Worship is the bridge that connects us to that source of life.

In worship, we don't just acknowledge God—we experience Him. We surrender our cares, our doubts, and even our fears, trusting in His ability to carry us through. This surrender isn't a loss; it's the ultimate gain. It's in these moments that we experience His presence as our peace.

Discovering Joy Through Prayerful Worship

Worship is not confined to a single moment or Sunday morning routine—it's a lifestyle of constant communion with God. In these moments of worship, God reveals more of Himself to us, reminding us of His love and drawing us closer to Him. Just as deep friendships thrive on time and conversation, so does our relationship with God. The more we seek Him, the more He shares the secrets of His heart.

Jeremiah 33:3 beautifully captures this: *"Call to me and I will answer you and tell you great and mighty things, which you do not know."* Imagine that! Worship allows us to step into a conversation with God where He shares His thoughts and plans with us, like an intimate secret whispered between close friends. These divine revelations fill our hearts with joy, reminding us that our true fulfillment comes not from circumstances or accomplishments but from Him alone.

Isn't it incredible how accessible this joy is? In a world that often complicates happiness, God simplifies it: "Call on Me." Through prayerful worship, we tune our hearts to hear His voice, sense His presence, and experience a joy that surpasses understanding.

Redefining Worship: It's More Than Church Songs

For many, worship is linked to church services or special gatherings. While those moments are meaningful, they're only a glimpse of what worship truly is. Worship can become the atmosphere of our daily lives.

What if, instead of limiting worship to a scheduled time or place, we embraced it as a lifestyle? Imagine living with a heart constantly postured in surrender to God, where praise flows naturally and the melody of heaven surrounds all you do and become. This might seem like a lofty goal, but with intentionality and practice, it's possible.

God reveals Himself in everyday moments, not just in church. Those seemingly random "coincidences" are often what I like to call "God kisses"—gentle reminders of His presence. It might be a kind word from a stranger, the beauty of a sunrise, or a perfectly timed answer to prayer. In these moments, joy isn't something we strive for; it finds us.

The knowledge that the Creator of the universe delights in spending time with us is awe-inspiring. How can that truth not bring about a smile on our faces and the greatest joy? With intention, worship can become the very air that we breathe; it's the heart of the Father to be this close to us through the Holy Spirit who lives inside us. He wants us to abide in Him; this means we are with Him constantly, all day, every day. He wants to be your best friend. It's the coolest thing ever to know that the one who created you wants to be that close to you and never leave you or forsake you, but the choice is up to us. I want to choose Him every day and every hour. I pray that it will be your heart's desire as well. Because that's where you will find the greatest joy of all, in the Love of the one who created and adores you.

Worship Through Our Work: A Surprising Source of Joy

Here's where worship takes an interesting turn—Worship extends beyond singing and prayer—it can even include our work. Colossians 3:23-24 reminds us: *"Whatever you do, work at it with all your heart, as working for the Lord, not for human masters."*

When we approach our work as an act of worship, it transforms even mundane tasks into opportunities to glorify God. Suddenly, our jobs aren't just about deadlines or paychecks—they become offerings to the Father, and in that offering, we find incredible joy.

This mindset shift is powerful. Imagine starting Monday mornings with the excitement of serving God through your work. Stress loses its grip when we see our efforts as acts of devotion. And here's the amazing part: God blesses our work when we do it with a heart of worship. Using the gifts He's given us to fulfill His purposes brings Him glory—and in turn, He blesses us abundantly. How amazing is that? You were created to bring glory to the Father through your gifts and talents, your unique design created to showcase something wonderful about the Father on the earth. You are to be a city on a hill that shines so bright that others run to come see why it's so lit up out there. What is making that "one" so different and special? You're designed to point people to Jesus by how you live, move, and do things differently in the world. We do this in our everyday going and coming, through our regular day and seemingly mundane tasks, we should point people to something greater within us. We should point people to want to worship the creator of all things. So, whatever you do, do it to the glory of the King!

Surrendering to His Plan: A Pathway to Joy

When we surrender to God's plan for our lives, joy begins to flow abundantly in every area. This surrender shifts our perspective, transforming worship from a momentary act into a lifestyle. When we worship God through our work and daily lives, we become carriers of His glory—not just for ourselves, but for those around us.

The beauty of being a glory carrier is that it's full of joy, and not only that, joy is contagious. A life aligned with God's will radiates joy, touching everyone we encounter. As John 15:11 reminds us: *"These things I have spoken to you, that My joy may remain in you, and that your joy may be full."* True joy, birthed from worship and surrender, is not superficial or dependent on circumstances. Instead, it's rooted in an unshakable connection with the Father.

Even in trials, worship keeps our spirit joyful because we trust in God's sovereignty, knowing that He works all things together for good (Romans 8:28). The good, the bad, and the ugly are working for our good. For those who love God and are called according to his purpose. In order to receive these blessings, we must come to a place of complete surrender. Surrender is relinquishing our will to pick up the will of the Father. This form of surrender requires trust and belief that what God has for you is better than what we could ever imagine. This surrender takes faith; even the smallest mustard seed faith is enough until He increases it. Because surrendering to His plans and purpose for our lives is the best decision we could ever make. Even when it seems impossible. It's here we enter into a true adventure, the one that leads us straight into a life of freedom and joy, and it's in this place we find out it was worth every sacrifice we may have been

required to relinquish to achieve this great reward. For He is our great reward…Amen!

Joy Through Constant Communion with God

In 1 Thessalonians 5:16-18, we are given a straightforward yet profound guide for living a joy-filled life: *"Rejoice always, pray constantly, give thanks in everything; for this is God's will for you in Christ Jesus."*

This threefold approach—rejoicing, praying, and giving thanks—creates a pathway to joy. Yet, in the busyness of life, it's easy to overlook these simple instructions.

When we do, stress and overwhelm often take joy's place.

However, God's will for us is to live in constant communion with Him. Through worship and prayer, we tap into a source of joy that is unstoppable, even in the most challenging times. Authentic praise and genuine worship unlock this abundant life, allowing us to experience joy regardless of our circumstances.

Let's make it our daily goal to worship in Spirit and in Truth (John 4:24). In doing so, we'll find that the joy we've been searching for has been waiting all along—in the heart of the Father, ready to overflow into our lives.

JOY NUGGET

Real and authentic JOY begins in TRUE WORSHIP of the one who created you. It's about abiding; being with the Father and desiring to know Him more. It's not dependent on what's happening around you but what's happening inside you. It's about drawing closer to His heart and learning of His love for you. **True joy comes from knowing you are loved unconditionally** and fully in the beloved.

DRAWING CLOSER

Jesus wants us to walk with him so closely that we know His thoughts towards us. Where we know what He wants us to do each day. He wants to speak to us about everything! All our concerns and those around you. He wants us to reflect His goodness and spread joy and love everywhere we go, so the world can see Him. As disciples, we represent Him on the earth. This should draw others to want to know Him. Your life will become a question that others ask: "What do they have … that I'm missing?" Then you can say, "It's not what you're missing but who…His name is Yeshua/Jesus!" Amen.

Scripture Reading (John 4)

Let's Pray:

Heavenly Father,

Thank You for giving us hearts that long to worship You in Spirit and in Truth. Thank You for being the Spirit of Truth, leading us into all truth. Stir within us a hunger and thirst for more of You. Teach us how to seek You through worship in the midst of our daily lives.

May worship become as natural as breathing, and may each breath remind us of how close You are and how dependable You are at every moment. Let Your love be the focus of our days and may all we do glorify You as an act of worship.

In Jesus' mighty name, Amen.

Thank you taking this journey with me ...

I pray you find your Joy in the never-ending, relentless **LOVE** of God. His goodness is always pursuing us, and He desires for you to know Him more deeply than you can imagine.

May your JOY always be rooted in HIM!

> *"God is **SPIRIT**, and those who **WORSHIP HIM** must worship in Spirit and in Truth."*
>
> John 4:24 (CSB)

Reflection & Revelation to Remember

www.ingramcontent.com/pod-product-compliance
Lightning Source LLC
LaVergne TN
LVHW030241250326
834688LV00047B/1760